NINE DAYS

Living With My Soul Wide Open
After Violent Trauma

MICHELLE RENEE

To respect the privacy of certain individuals involved in my journey, some names, locations, and dates may have been changed or omitted.

NINE DAYS
Learning to Live With My Soul Wide Open After Violent Trauma Book Cover & Jacket Design by VERB Media Group, Inc. Cover Photos: Adobe Stock Photos

ISBN E-Book: 979-8-9878414-0-2
ISBN Paperback: 979-8-9878414-2-6
ISBN Hardcover: 979-8-9878414-1-9

1. Renee, Michelle, 2023 —Memoir—Survival. 2. Self-Help —Inner Child. 3. Woman's Inspirational Spirituality

First Edition 2023

ALSO BY MICHELLE RENEE

Held Hostage

Lifetime Movie: Held Hostage
(Writer & Assoc. Producer)

NINE DAYS

DEDICATION

This is for you, my angel. It is all for you. Forever.
To my siblings, the Wolf Pack, I love you deeply.

CONTENTS

AUTHORS NOTE

To write this book I sat for countless hours in my chaise lounge chair next to the window overlooking San Diego, classical piano and guitar softly playing in the background, typing on my laptop. When I wasn't there, I was at my small glass dining room table scouring through all of the video footage I had taken on the nine-day solo quest to Eagle River, Alaska to get back to my daughter. I watched each moment of the tapes I had recorded on the road, from picnic benches to inside my tent. On the edge of the bed in a dingy motel room, and inside my car as I drove. I looked back on journal entries, and court transcripts, studied photos, and took some of what had been written previously in my first book, Held Hostage.

NINE DAYS is the telling of my story, our story, up to an incredible moment in April 2022 that truly brought healing full circle. This work is focused on what has always been most important to me: healing, relationships, and learning to live freely without the chains of trauma. Not "true crime". This is about so much more than the crime itself. This is about the resilience of the human spirit, a mother's love, transformation, redemption, and self-discovery that began on a 4200-mile trek into the Alaskan wilderness.

I chose to change some of the names of those involved and omit others out of respect and privacy.

Your task is not to seek for love, but merely to seek and find all the barriers within yourself that you have built against it.

— Rumi

PROLOGUE

'Bones' was his street name. His gang moniker. He was serving multiple consecutive life sentences plus 32 years in the maximum security facility on the edge of San Francisco, San Quentin State Prison, for what he had done to us. His chains and bars, his prison, were different from ours. What he, and his co-defendants, ripped from us created invisible chains that took years, and miles, to unlock and allow to drop to the ground to heal forward without the choke-hold of hate cutting off our oxygen supply. The kind of prison we were in for so long was as harsh as a bitter, cold Alaskan winter.

It was a blisteringly hot day in July driving towards my destination on a nearly 4200-mile solo journey on gravel, dirt, and black tar. The challenges I had faced and overcome, not only in my life since childhood but on this road trip as yellow lines streaked by, were softening me somehow. I began to wonder how someone could get to a place so desperate that they believed their only option was to attack and destroy the lives of a mother and her only child. "What happened to them that took them so far into the dark underbelly of the world that they chose to do something so horrific?

That question, and many more, began to surface on the open road from San Diego to Eagle River, Alaska. A nine-day journey to get back to where my daughter was waiting for me. Her birthday was in nine days. I had to make it there, no matter what. I promised her I would be there. I set out to get from point A to point B on a paper map, up the coast and through the open tundra of the Yukon on miles of unpaved road with my dog Haley, little money or food, driving a small SUV with 104 thousand miles already on the engine. But I wasn't doing this because I had to or because I wanted to. I was doing what I knew I was being called to do, driven to do, fear and all.

We had made it out alive but that just meant we were still breathing. But living? Were we really "alive"? What did that even mean anymore? Who was I now? How do I be a mother to a child with so much trauma? How do I stop all the noise in my mind that is taking over as I beg myself to do anything to stop it? As I lay curled up in a ball at 3:00 AM, a message came. I could feel a presence in my room. A glow. I listened.

"It's all going to be all right. Just rest. Rest and trust."

Then another. I kept listening. I began to write. I couldn't stop. It was as though something else was taking over. It was just pouring out of me and I thought someday, she would read it all. It was for her. All of it. Mountains of memories and thoughts.

Another divine download happened while exploring ice caves and trekking on the Matanuska Glacier in Alaska. The message was clear. I was beginning to trust this deep inner guidance. This time, it was louder and a massive calling that would change everything.

Six days later I was in my old, small burgundy SUV headed northbound on I-5 with San Diego disappearing in my rear view mirror as the sun set on a balmy summer evening in July. I had nine days to get back to her. Nine days to listen. Nine days to learn, let go, heal and discover. I had nine days to learn how to live with my soul wide open.

The setting sun was casting a soft golden glow on the rolling hills to my right as cars whisked by. I didn't know what was ahead of me as I glanced in the rear view mirror watching the city I love slowly fade with the sun.

I gripped the wheel, merged into the fast lane, and pressed harder on the gas pedal with my toes until the speedometer hit 85 MPH on a road trip of a lifetime that sparked the unexpected. The extraordinary.

PART 1
THE NAKED TRUTH

Help me conquer these fears that lie to me. Help me show them the tears that fall when I'm alone. I only fall when I'm alone. Help me stand in front of you in the light of naked truth. Help me climb these mountains I've built around me so that I can be everything I was born to be.

1

PISMO BEACH

The sun had long set on the beachside landscape. Headlights were casting long shadows across the cracked asphalt as a cool breeze whispered through an abandoned gas station. I squinted my eyes and leaned in toward the steering wheel. My eyes were getting heavy and I needed a place to crash.

The faded arrow was pointing to a campground just off the highway. Taking a deep breath, I repositioned my hands on the worn steering wheel, trembling with a mixture of anticipation and fear. My mind wandered back to the moment that had shattered us. The weight of grief pressed against my chest, but I refused to let it suffocate me any longer. This journey *had to be* my way back to myself, to reclaiming control amidst the chaos.

My headlights lit up the sign that read "Campground full" as I pulled in just past midnight. I entered the campground ignoring the sign and inched toward the security check-in point. I looked over at Haley, my four-legged companion, and dimmed my headlights.

I had arrived at the small beachside campground in Pismo Beach after hours on the road. My tires were stirring up well-maintained gravel as I crept through the roads that gently curve around the landscape. I was looking for a spot to stop and try to blend in amongst the colorful tents spread out in the open, grassy spaces. It was the first day of my new life, whatever that meant.

A few lights lined the small winding road past campsites with smoldering, flickering flames and glowing embers from the evening fires. I smelled burning wood and salt in the air and saw glimpses of twinkling lanterns as I searched for somewhere to pull up and pitch my tiny one-person army tent. Scents of the outdoors enveloped me as I drove across the narrow road dimly lit by my parking lights. Finally, I spotted an already occupied campsite near an open parking space. It would have to do for tonight. I had to sleep somewhere. My eyes wouldn't stay open much longer.

I parked the car and told my pit bull, Haley, to be quiet. I used my parking lights to read the small, faded details that would help me pitch the tent. The paper was worn and hard to read. I tried everything I could to make it work. No luck. Frustrated and drained, I gave up and began pulling items out from behind the driver's seat and stacking them against the car: a folding chair, a duffle bag of clothes, anything bulky that made me unable to completely recline. Finally, the seat clicked all the way back.

Getting caught in a parking space next to someone's campsite had not been in the plan. The sound of dry dog food hitting the silver metal bowl seemed too loud. Haley inhaled her food, lapped up half a bowl of water, and made a mad dash to the grass area nearby, dragging me behind clinging to her leash.

After draping towels over the front windows, I cracked one back window slightly for a little bit of air, locked all the doors, and covered myself head to toe with a thick cotton blanket. I prayed for sleep to come as I shut my eyes, a canister of pepper spray clutched in my hand. Haley curled up in the passenger seat and I began to drift into a slumber, my mind on my daughter, Breea.

3 Days Earlier

It had seemed like the worst punishment in the world to leave Breea, fly home to San Diego, and then drive all alone up the west coast of the US from San Diego through Canada and the rugged terrain of the Yukon Territory and into the Alaska wilderness. I had been warned that a large part of what is known as the AL-Can highway was mostly unpaved. We had arrived four days earlier. I flew her there to get her out of harm's way after receiving a call from the FBI saying we should probably get out of dodge. I wasn't waiting for the risk assessment they were going to do that might take weeks. I called her grandmother and got the green light to fly there, and get Breea settled in and I was going to figure the rest out later. I wasn't expecting those four days to turn into a calling in my soul I could not ignore.

Leaving her at the airport promising I would be back reminded me of the last time I promised I would be back. Only this time she wasn't duct taped in a closet and I wasn't being forced to leave her at gunpoint.

I was about to pass through security feeling her tiny fingers nestled into my palm. I turned to her, knelt and gave her a hard kiss on her forehead, and hugged her tight. I didn't want to let go. Was I making a mistake leaving her here with her Grandmother without me? What if she fell apart the minute I left? What if *I* did?

I tore myself away and put my pinky out. "Let's make a pinky promise," I said. A big lump in my throat was choking me.

"Okay Mama," she said softly.

"I'll be back for your birthday. Pinky."

"Pinky Mama?"

"Yes, angel. Pinky."

We locked fingers. I pulled her close and melted into her.

When I approached the gate, I turned to her reluctantly, waving good bye. Of course, Breea did not want me to leave, but she knew she was safe with her grandmother until I could get back to her.

"I'll be back before you know it, sweetie!" I told her.

"I love you."

"I love you more."

"No, me."

This is a game we play.

"No, it's me for sure," I replied.

"No, both Mama. We love each other the same."

"Okay. You're right. Both. We love each other the same. The exact same."

I waved and blew a ridiculous amount of air kisses her way. It somehow made our separation feel less desperate and sad and more about looking forward to getting back. It was July 3rd, five days after we'd arrived in Eagle River, Alaska when I tearfully faced the gate. I walked along the ramp to the plane, trying to quiet my mind. "What if she keeps having nightmares? What if she gets sick and I can't get back to help her? What if she gets hurt and I can't be there to pick her up and put on her bandages?" The what if's were stacking up.

I boarded the plane, frustrated that I hadn't been able to stop the evil in the world from harming my daughter and me. I hated that I had failed to keep her safe from *them*. Was I to blame for the trauma that plagued her now? Had I been too busy to realize I was being stalked? Reeling with guilt, I staggered to my window seat. In 13 days, Breea would be turning eight. How would I make her life work for her? How could I make our life normal again?

I rested my head against the cold Plexiglas window and closed my eyes. I had no idea who was sitting on the seats beside me and I was too tormented and confused to care. When the plane lifted off, I stared out over the magnificent snow-capped mountain peaks and gratefully, I drifted off to sleep for an hour or two.

The next day, back in San Diego, I organized a front yard giveaway. It was a veritable 'Sale of the Century' with a road trip donation jar for anyone who wanted to contribute to my imminent journey North. Hand-scribbled paper signs with the words "FREE" or "MAKE AN OFFER" dangled from furniture, old bikes, second-hand clothing, and lamps in the front yard of the rental we had lived in for a few short months. It didn't take long for the crowds to arrive and swoop up my old stuff, things that had meant something. Now they didn't. All that mattered was getting back to Breea. When the sale was over, I would be rid of everything I didn't want, need or care about.

In the late afternoon, my sister arrived with her husband and their pick-up truck to take some sentimental things I couldn't part with the set of China my ex-husband had given me on our first anniversary, the refurbished treasure chest that held my pregnancy diary, pictures of the sonogram and the dress that Breea wore home from the hospital. I stroked the baby blue dress, trimmed with white lace that I had wrapped her in when I first took her home. In nine days, I'd be seeing her again, hearing her sweet, soft voice, touching her soft pale cheeks, and kissing her.

I went to my landlady, paid her what I owed, and stuffed nearly five hundred dollars in my pocket for the trip. It wasn't much but it had to be enough. I cleared the last food items out of the refrigerator and threw them in a white and blue mini cooler. Then I grabbed the canister of pepper spray I'd purchased weeks before and put a leash around Haley's neck. She was a white and brown pit bull my sister gave me so I would have a companion and extra security on the road. If my car broke down, I'd be forced to seek help from strangers. That scared me more than anything else, but I had sweet-tempered Haley who could turn into 'Fido the Ripper' at a moment's notice.

I called my brother Dave. He said he could hear my determination and he knew I was doing exactly what I needed to do what I was being led to do. Then I went to see my best friend, Kristi. She walked through the glass double doors of an office building and straight to my car parked outside. She leaned up against the back of my compact SUV. "Are you *really* going to do this?" she asked as she reached her arms out to hug me.

"I *have* to," I told her.

It was impossible for her to understand.

I hugged her tight, kissed her cheek and I hit the road to Alaska. On July 6th, as the sun was setting in the western sky, Kristi watched me drive away in the packed mini SUV.

I watched a magnificent sunset as my hands gripped the wheel. I turned left towards the on-ramp and watched my broken dreams disappear in the rearview mirror as I headed North to the Interstate 5 freeway. I was all alone with my new four-legged companion. Goodbye old home. Goodbye.

2

LEARNING TO TRUST

A knock on the car window startled me awake just after Sunrise. I peered my head out from under the blanket to see the man whose campsite I'd crept up next to. He looked stunned when he saw me, as though he'd expected anyone other than a woman with box-dyed hair and her dog. I slowly pushed aside the towel I had hung to cover the window the night before that had partially slipped down on one side. The light stung my eyes and I explained my situation briefly. Thankfully, he allowed me to stay at the edge of his campsite until I could pull myself together.

He offered to watch my stuff while I found a place to brush my teeth and hair. I hadn't trusted anyone in so long, I didn't know how to anymore. My mind was in a fierce battle, giving me opposite orders. It was between "You're ready to try," and "Run for your life. "In that moment, I knew I had to decide whether to trust a stranger or take off. But even in my terrified state, I remembered that I was on this trip for a reason. I took a deep breath, looked the strange man square in the eye, and said, "That would be great. Thank you."

I headed for the .25 cent shower, continuously looking back to be sure my dog and car were safe. I gripped my towel and walked quickly. The cement shower stall was clean and basic. I waited for the water to heat up before I stripped down and stepped in barefooted. The water poured over my body and I could hear the drain sucking up the suds that trickled down my legs. I washed my hair and braced myself against the gray pitted walls of the stall. Suddenly, I was back there…again.

6:00 AM November 21, 2000

"Go take a fuckin' shower," the stocky man had ordered me, grabbing my sore and bruised wrists. "Do all the things you normally do to get ready for work. Fix your hair and wear them business clothes you got."

A metallic taste burned my throat as I catapulted straight up in my bed in a cold sweat. This was not a dream. My eyes welled up and I tightened my hold on Breea who was rustling beside me. I glanced at the sheer white fabric that covered my windows undulated in the morning breeze that blew up from the canyon below. I thought those curtains were romantic when I bought them. Each morning, I'd gently awakened and could see the ocean right through them, a patch of crystal clear blueness that lay beyond the heavy stone retaining wall in the front of the home I loved so much. If this were a dream I could go back and fix it but last night there was no horror movie. It was real, in my face, and unavoidable, as if it were a regular day.

"Breea, honey. Wake up baby," I whispered. I inhaled her hair and caressed her soft skin. Her eyes opened more turquoise green than the Caribbean ocean. If this were my time to die, so be it, but it was not her time. No child should be put through this kind of pain. She was only seven years old, for God's sake! Rage flew up my spine. I hardened into a cold ball of ice, a stoic determination rising from my fury. I would get through this with no mistakes. That was the mindset I needed, the absolute commitment to do everything they told me to do perfectly. Then I would help put the pathetic creeps behind bars for the rest of their lives.

I swept Breea up in my arms. "I'm too scared to cry, Mommy," she said. Tears streaked my face as I headed for the shower.

"Where do you think you're taking her?" the man asked. The talker's voice was shaky, on the edge of panic, and a lot less confident than it had sounded last night.

"She and I always shower together in the morning," I said. It was a lie and I hoped they hadn't been watching me closely enough or early enough in the mornings to know it. I just couldn't let go of her, not yet. Not now.

He let me take her into the bathroom. I started to close the door and he shoved my arm away, watching our every move as I turned on the shower. I slid my clothes to the floor and concealed Breea's body with my own, trying to use the Plexiglas door as a shield. The warm water poured over us and I raised my eyes to the ceiling, trying to get my wits about me. I was not tired, even though I hadn't slept in over 24 hours. My adrenaline was pumping, terror coursed through me and I let the water mask the tears that were running down my face. I could make out the gunman's shadowy figure through the steamed glass panel of the metal-trimmed shower door.

Breea clung to my naked hips, the wet droplets on her long eyelashes, falling to the tile floor. The man tapped on the shower door with his gun and we both jumped.

"We ain't got all day," he said. "Let's go."

I stroked Breea's hair back from her face and turned off the water. We stepped out of the shower, exposed. The door hinge complained with a squeaking sound. Breea stayed behind the shower door as I reached for a towel.

The gunman stared right at us, his feet about shoulder width apart as he gripped his black handgun. Breea stood behind me, peering out from behind my right side. I rushed to cover her with a bath towel and then I covered my own. I wanted to crumble to the floor in a ball and scream for mercy, but that would do nothing for either Breea or me. I resented these men for how badly my little girl would feel about life and men after this.

And what about me? I would never feel the same about men, my body, or my privacy. I closed my eyes tightly, massaging my sore wrists and putting the towel up to my face with both hands as Breea clung tightly to my leg. I tried to focus on what I had to do next, moving with a crawling numbness, feeling less than human as I found familiar clothes for us to wear.

"Turn around and pull up your shirt," the ringleader harshly ordered.

Breea was fully clothed now, sitting close to me on the bathroom count er. I pulled up my shirt, grasping onto the cold tile countertop with my hands while the men used duct tape to strap red dynamite sticks to my back. They dug sharply into my spine and the foul smell of his body odor nauseated me. He was taping me so tightly, my rib cage felt constricted. "Please loosen it," I pleaded. "I can't breathe."

He ignored me and approached my daughter with two more sticks of dynamite. I wanted to stab him with something – anything to keep him from touching my baby. When he and the largest of the three men lifted my daughter's shirt to tape explosives on her tiny back, if someone had put a gun in my hand at that moment, I would have shot them both dead.

Breea was shaking as her hands gripped the edges of the toilet for bal ance while they finished taping the dynamite. She whimpered softly. "Mommy, it hurts so bad. Right here." she pointed to her ribs. "I can't breathe. Please make them take it off, please."

I turned to the faceless man and began to scream, "Loosen the fucking tape on her. Please!"

He gestured to the tall man to re-tape Breea. "Now shut up and wear this," he said, throwing a loose-fitting tan sports jacket at me. He'd chosen it from my closet while I was in the shower. Trance-like, I put it on. "Now turn around," he said. I turned my back toward him. "Yeah, that works," he mused, referring to the fact that the jacket hid the explosives from view. "Now go sit in the living room. I'll tell you when it's time."

I took Breea's hand and we walked slowly into the living room with the burdens on our backs.

"If you try to take off the tape or the dynamite," the talker reminded me, "the thing will detonate. We wouldn't want the little girl to be an orphan, would we?"

"What did they put on me, Mommy?" Breea asked.

"Just something to keep track of you, sweetie." I didn't want her to know. I wanted to make it unreal for her but it *was* real and all I could do was pray we didn't end up in a million pieces. I sat helplessly on the living room couch with duct tape cutting into my ribs and explosives on my back.

It was almost time.

3

BE BRAVE

July 7, 2001

The shower suddenly stopped in the tiny campground cement stall. Drops from the shower head above landed one by one on my scalp and made their way down my back. My naked body was chilled and it took me a moment to realize where I was. I didn't want to use another 25 cents. I felt sick to my stomach and reached for my towel. I couldn't get all of the suds off my body but it didn't matter. I needed to get on the road. I reached for my clothes and pulled my shirt over my head. I couldn't shake off the images that kept replaying in my mind. I looked into the mirror. "Breea," I thought to myself, trying to make the flashbacks stop.

"Are you okay in there?" a woman's voice asked, alerting me that I had been in the bathroom longer than I had expected. I looked in the mir ror again, wiped my face, pulled on my jeans, forced my damp feet into day-old socks, and crammed them into my hiking boots. Then I made a b-line back to the safety of my small, burgundy SUV.

"Can I offer you a cup of coffee?" the man asked as I flung open the driver's side door.

"No, no thanks," I said as I motioned for Haley to get in. "Um, okay. Well, thank you, sir." The look on his face was either confusion or worry, or a mix of both. I shut the door and locked it quickly. Then I drove away, heading toward the on-ramp of Interstate 5 north. It was day two of my road trip and I was already praying for the guts and determination to keep going.

I was south of Napa when I needed to fill my gas tank and my stomach. The 101 was a slow way to travel. Traffic was jammed like a parking lot and I felt like I was falling behind. The sun would be setting in an hour or so, and I wanted to cover as much ground as I could before it got dark. Then at 10:00 p.m., it began to rain. I pulled into a gas station for fuel and a cup of hot cocoa. But when I got back to the car to get in beside Haley, I realized she had put her paw up on the door near the window in her excitement seeing me return to the car, and hit the lock. I was locked out. The keys dangled in the ignition, Haley's tail wagged a mile a minute, and I had to brave the rain again and run back into the mini-mart.

The attendant, a Middle Eastern man, spoke almost no English. I walked back outside into the soaking rain, terrified, seeing the bogey man in the shadows, wondering what on earth to do when three men walked out of the store, looking like they were returning from a fishing trip. I caught my breath, tried to stop myself from shaking, and asked for help. They called the local fire department. "They'll be here in ten minutes, ma'am," they said.

Ten minutes. My mind flashed back to that terrible morning. "You have ten minutes to say whatever you need to say to your girl," he told me. "Remember, if you mess up, you'll never see her alive again."

Ten minutes to say everything? Impossible. How do you put every word, every emotion, and every dream for your daughter into ten minutes? How do you explain all the things you wish you could take back or undo or do again? How do you say it all? Ten minutes.

7:20 AM November 21, 2000

I leaned in as close to her ears as I could get, trying to keep our words private. "You are so special, baby," I whispered. "You're everything I ever dreamed of when I chose to be a Mommy. God made you perfect for me, did you know that? I love you more than I can say and I'm so proud of you. You are my hero, my angel, and guess what? I'll be back to get you as soon as I can. Okay? It's all going to be fine."

My mind was playing worst-case scenarios. What if I fainted or vomited and couldn't carry out the plan? Would they kill us? What if there wasn't enough money in the vault that day? What if they panicked and got trigger-happy? What if they detonated the dynamite right now and we exploded all over the house?

"I know you're gonna do all the stuff they told you to, Mommy." Breea's voice reminded me that I was losing my concentration. I focused on her beautiful eyes. "You're tough and brave, remember?" she said to me.

"So are you, sweetie," I answered. "We're going to get through this together, right?"

"Right," she said weakly.

"Remember our song," I said. Together forever just you and me. She joined in. *Together forever that's the way it's meant to be.*

"That's us, Mommy."

"Yup, that's us and no matter what, it's true. We're together forever. I love you a million times plus eternity."

"Be brave Mommy." Those were the words I'd told *her* time and again, and now she was repeating them to me. *Be brave.* I hugged her, rocking back and forth, kissing her long and hard on her forehead and cheek, my arms wrapped tightly around her body and face as I felt the bulging torture sticks strapped to her narrow back.

"That's enough," the man said, his ugly mask lighting up in the glow of the rising sun. "Take her into her bedroom. NOW!"

We walked into Breea's bedroom.

"Put her in the closet!" an angry voice ordered. I clutched Breea to my leg as gently as I could. Any movement felt dangerous with the dyna mite on our bodies. I gazed into the dark closet. I couldn't allow her to sit in there like that. "Can I give her something to keep her occupied in there, just a little something, you know anything, a crayon, and paper…please?"

"Make it quick."

I searched desperately for a pad of paper, a pencil, or crayons – any thing she could use to write or draw, to keep herself busy. Her Game Boy, the one we were playing with just hours before, was still in the living room.

"Here baby," I said, handing her a pad of paper that was next to her bed. "Draw a pretty picture or write Mommy a note. I'll be back as soon as I can, Sweetie."

"Be brave Mommy." she reminded me. Again.

I held my pinky out. "Pinky promise angel." I said, trying to convince myself. I felt her soft, small finger wrap around mine and then slip away. I stood slowly and we used our secret sign language to say, "I love you for eternity."

Breea began to *really* cry. "Mommy, no. Don't leave, Mommy, please..."

The stalker shoved me towards the door and my daughter's cries faded as I became lifeless, mechanical. I walked out of the bedroom, leaving behind my daughter strapped with explosives, imprisoned in the clos et. She was counting on me to keep her alive.

A gloved hand gripped my arm as my daughter's screams faded. I felt myself leaving my body. I was becoming a robot. He shoved me out the front door, sticking his gun into my side. I headed toward my Jeep as the door slammed behind me. I was preparing to die and he would never know my past, my violent childhood, and the things that I'd already survived . . .

10:35 p.m. July 7, 2001

A big red fire engine with lights flashing pulled up to rescue me from the massive downpour. They opened the car door in a jiffy and I thanked the sweet strangers profusely, got back in the car, and stared at Haley. I wanted to blame someone else for locking me out, but it wasn't Haley's fault. It was mine. I'd never taken responsibility for the wrongs in my life. I was used to running away, praying that my troubles wouldn't follow me. Of course, they always did until now out on the road alone. I was doing it differently by taking inventory and it wasn't easy since I was viewing everything differently since that night. Even things that seemed insignificant held life lessons, now that my eyes and soul were being peeled open.

I could see that if I hadn't been locked out of the car, I would not have needed to ask for help. This was #2 on the list of lessons in trust and faith on the trip so far. Looking on the bright side of things took on a whole new meaning as the rain ferociously battered my car. I knew there was no way I was going to be able to set up camp. The rain was nonstop. I weaved in and out of parking lots, running into motels to ask how much they would charge for one night. There were plenty of vacancies, but not a single room that would allow dogs. My eyes were stinging as I circled the parking lot at the last boutique hotel that refused to allow Haley inside with me.

"Not ideal, Haley," I said as I rubbed her head. I found a parking spot in between two cars in the back of the parking lot. Just like the night before, I did my best to get my seat to recline, shoved towels into small cracks in the window, and covered my head with a blanket. The rain pelting the roof of my car somehow felt like a lullaby. It reminded me of the time I had stolen my friend Bob's truck to have a place to sleep. I was a teenager with no driver's license. His Mom found me sneaking in through his bedroom window and sleeping in his room. Anywhere was better than going back to live with my parents and the suffocating dysfunction. We weren't romantically involved. He wanted us to be and I knew it. I knew that with Bob I could get away with anything, including taking his truck and my large green plastic Hefty bag full of everything I owned and driving until I could barely see straight. I eventually parked and slept across the bench seat with my head on my be longings. I returned the truck two weeks later and never saw Bob again.

Rain fell creating a soft pitter-patter sound as droplets hit the roof and windshield that had an almost magical effect. My body was fatigued already. I could see the rain passing through the rays of light streaming down from the parking lot light. I pulled the blanket up over my face and shut my eyes, desiring morning to come, hopeful for what tomorrow may bring.

4

THE MIDDLE CHILD

July 8, 2001

"Grandma got me a map, Mommy," Breea said ecstatically when I called her before hitting the road to Napa. She was tracking my progress on a map.

"That is so cool!" I said. "I'm on my way, Prin!"

"Tell me where you are and I'll look at the map Mama."

"I'm close to Napa, sweetie. I'll be back in seven days." When I hung up, I wondered if I would actually make it. "This is your plan, not mine, God," I said out loud. I drove towards the center of California, taking in everything as I wove in and out of quaint towns along the road, stopping at coffee shops for a cup of java. Something unexpected was happening. I was reveling in the fact that I was free to be simply myself on the road. No one knew my name. No one knew my past. There was no one to judge me, blame me, or see me as someone I was not. If they did, I was unconcerned. I had no one to worry about, protect or impress, no one to convince, and no more stern-looking suits and shiny shoes interrogating me as if I were a criminal.

I needed strength to withstand the struggles ahead to teach me how to function in the world once again, fear and all. I sailed along Route 1, the Pacific Coast Highway, that stretched from San Diego to the furthest points North. I looked at the breathtaking beauty of the sea side with its glorious cliffs leading down to crashing waves. I stopped occasionally to enjoy the view and take more pictures. I kept telling myself that it was safe to get out of the car, although I didn't believe it most of the time.

I had to find a way to charge my video camera battery and I spotted a Target sign. I didn't want to miss capturing my trip to share with Breea after I arrived back in Alaska. My scrappy days as a teen runaway had taught me to think outside the box. There had to be an outlet some where. When I pulled up to the double doors and stopped for shoppers to cross in front of me I noticed a kid's mini stationary train ride that moved back and forth for a minute or two. There were no kids any where in sight so I grabbed my camera and the power cord and headed for the little train. Behind it was a power source. I plugged in my cam era and hid it as far back as I could so no one would see it. I returned to my car, grabbed the bills I needed to pay and I sat on a cold bench with a pen, my checkbook, and a few stamps.

Thirty minutes later, I mailed my bills, went to Target, and bought a gift for Breea. It was a cheap yellow scooter that was 75% off! I paid $2.50. I knew her face would light up when I arrived on her birthday with a bright yellow gift and tons of hugs. My camera was charged up, no one had stolen it, and I figured out a way to fit the birthday present in my car along with a volleyball I scored that had been on sale too.

When I got back on the road, I turned the 70s music station up and rolled my window down.

She's a lady.
Whoa, whoa, whoa.
She's a lady.
Talkin' about that little lady,
And the lady is mine.

Tom Jones was belting out one of his hits as I took the curves through the lush vineyards of Napa. I smiled remembering how much my Mom loved him. I mean *really* loved him. Celebrity crush was putting it mildly. There was no doubt I inherited her boy craziness and love of music. I reached for the black volume dial and cranked it up. The wind was warm on my face and my left hand dangled when it wasn't wrestling to keep my hair out of my eyes.

Yeah yeah yeah. She's a Lady Listen to me baby, She's a Lady...

San Diego, 1972

"Shhhhh. You're staying home from school today," my Mom had whispered. "I'll come to get you when the coast is clear." She headed for the kitchen as my dad screamed, "Linda, I need more coffee!" He was sitting three feet from the pot of Folgers, lighting up a Pall Mall unfiltered cancer stick that triggered my severe asthma growing up. The mixture of burning tobacco with its poisonous gas, particles, and chemicals landed me in a hospital bed surrounded by thick plastic, mist, and nurses, sometimes for weeks.

When the coast was clear, it was just Mom and me. It seemed like she was superhuman. Seven kids, multiple jobs, and an abusive husband, and there was never a dirty dish or pile of dirty laundry in sight. She was the hardest-working person I ever saw. She was the team Mom for my brother's baseball teams, the best scorekeeper you'd ever seen in the stands with her yellow #2 pencil, and faded green scorebook. But she was damaged.

On days when I got to stay home with her, the music played all day. We listened to Barry Manilow, Neil Diamond, Elvis, and Tom Jones while we danced around the living room, moments I wished would last forever.

When I was seven my father drove away from our modest home out side of Boston in an old beat-up Ford with my surrogate Uncle Dave beside him. Leaving behind seven children and his broken, battered wife, my father was headed for Southern California. The next morning was quiet. He was gone. No yelling echoed through the halls and when I wandered into the kitchen, there was no smoke to escalate my asthma. There were only stale cigarette butts in full ashtrays and day old sheets of the Sports page strewn across the table. My dad, the man who called women "whores," and houseflies "little niggers," was gone.

The youngest of three girls, I was the middle child of seven. I grew up in a variety of houses that never seemed like homes, on nameless streets in nameless towns. That was how it felt anyway as each new location was ruined by my father's rigid control and raging outbursts. Born on the outskirts of Boston, when I was an infant, my asthma caused me to spend many months at various intervals in a plastic-tented hospital bed, showered with warm, sticky mists to open my throat. Gasping for breath, I got poked and prodded regularly by nurses in crisp white uniforms and white caps. I was isolated most of the time feeling for so long it was punishment. For what, I had no idea. After a childhood of long, uninterrupted silences, I developed a love of and need for solitude. Maybe that was why the road felt like where I belonged.

David, my father, an orphaned Boston street punk measuring in at five feet two inches on his tiptoes, walked like he was six feet tall, holding high his handsome swarthy Spanish-Portuguese face. A hard-working man with an insatiable bruised ego and an abandoned inner child, he believed in introducing his young children to the harsh reality of the world by beating it into us. He had slicked-back ebony hair and he acted like he was invincible. But on the inside, he was a fragile, lost little boy whose parents walked him into an orphanage, handed him over, and left.

When I learned to walk, I was aware from an early age that keeping my father calm by following his instructions, no matter how ridiculous they seemed, was of the utmost importance. The key to survival. As I grew, I learned to predict my father's moods, struggling to endure the harsh grip that dug deeply into my arm and the jab to my self-worth amid my mother's agonized weeping. I never talked back or disagreed with him. That was a sure ticket to abuse, and my mother couldn't stick up for me, or any of us for that matter. I knew that she wanted to tell him to stop. I could see it in her pale blue Irish eyes. But little did I know or understand that her silence was her attempt to avoid a beating of her own.

In this stifling and violent atmosphere, my self-esteem slowly deteriorated, leaving nothing but a critical voice hammering home themes sage to me that I was no good. Why else would he abuse me and call me names every time he got the chance? And why wouldn't my mother stop him? I tried to stay close to her when I was growing up. Those times she took us hiking or let me stay home from school so she and I could just dance around the living room was magic. But the good times were slim and our isolation from relatives came year after year until I was old enough to realize we didn't have a relationship of any kind with a grandparent or an aunt or uncle or cousins like most kids did. I fantasized that when I got married, I would give my children oodles of love, protection, a permanent home, and the joy of family. I thought I was in charge of my destiny and circumstances naiveté at its best.

Just like any other kid, I wanted to know I was loved and as the verbal and physical abuse continued to escalate, I tried harder and harder to make my parents proud of me. I wanted to be daddy's princess, but instead, I was witness to his violent rages and left to feel like a fourth of seven of my parents' mistakes.

Holidays in particular were a badly-played game in my opinion. Sure we smiled. Sure we acted happy and we ate big meals and opened presents under the tree. But we all knew that our gifts had been purchased with bad checks that my mother wrote. We also knew that soon enough, the electricity and gas would be turned off and my father would erupt. We tried to keep that out of our minds, but without fail, as soon as the shut-off notices would arrive, we'd be shivering, hungry, and wandering around in the dark...again.

The pattern was always the same, with a slight variation. We would start to feel somewhat hopeful when we were on our own until a month or two later when Mom, overwhelmed by raising seven children alone, would give in to the pressures of life without him. When the phone rang, she'd go running back to the promises that it would be different this time only to start the process all over again.

When I was eight we headed for the golden state of California. Within weeks of my dad bolting west, Mom had packed all seven of us into her tiny red hatchback car with a few of our most precious belongings. She put on a pair of cute white knickers, white dock sneakers, and a tank top, wrapped a bandanna around her head and we were off. I remember gazing out of the hatchback window with tears streaming down my face, mourning my childish treasures that now filled the green, overstuffed trash cans as a result of our sudden move. I tried to lose my sadness and fear in my mother's joy as she sang us radio tunes in the car and thrilled with her beautiful laughter that we heard so rarely. We were heading West, she told us, to be with my dad (and his demons) in his supposed newfound Paradise.

It was on that extended cross-country journey that I learned to love the open road. I savored the sense of freedom and I learned to swallow my tears, a hard-earned lesson. We would all need that kind of control to deal with what was to come when we reached our destination. But during the trip, even though we got lost constantly, my mom made jokes and sang songs to lighten the mood. The freeway ramps in the shape of the number eight were like roller coasters to me, as I had never seen so many bridges, ramps, and speeding automobiles. And Mom did not seem to be in that much of a hurry to get to Paradise, which was at best, a large unknown.

For her, the trip was filled with obstacles, like the time we broke down in the dead of the summer heat, smack dab in the middle of the huge state of Texas. We were seven screaming kids, making it even tougher on Mom who paced outside the car in her cute little outfit with her hands on her hips and a world of worry on her face. When a man in a ten-gallon cowboy hat pulled over to see if we needed some assistance, I fantasized about him sweeping Mom off her feet. I imagined his large, earthy, calloused hands stroking her flaming red hair as he kissed her, just like in a classic romance novel. He would ask us all to pile into his Suburban SUV and deliver us to his spectacular horse ranch where we would all live happily ever after, never reaching California at all. But my hopeful scenario played out differently in real life than it did in my fantasy.

The man in the hat went for a tow truck and rented us a car so we could make it to the nearest hotel. He paid the bill there, and although we didn't get to ride off into the sunset with him, we did get to take baths and spend the night in a decent room, sleeping in a real bed. In the morning, we were rested and ready to hit the road again, wondering whether the cowboy had been a mirage or a miracle. Either way, we were back on the road. California and my dad's unchecked rage were twenty-four hours away.

5

IT'S NOT THEM

The woman wailed as she laid into her horn like she was giving chest compressions in a CPR class.

"The light couldn't be greener,"

"Sorry," I said with a slight wave and moved through the intersection toward Main Street in Napa, California. When I stopped to photo graph the wineries that reminded me of old Italian villas, I had the feeling I was beginning to heal. I had a new sense of progress, relief, and hope away from emotional pain and hurt and towards a state of emotional well-being and peace. I felt lighter and more optimistic than I had in ages. There was a growing awareness of inner strength and resilience that were small signs of healing, encouragement, and motivation to continue.

To prove it to myself, I lived out a fantasy I'd envisioned a thousand times. I took off my shoes and ran between long rows of vines that were waving in the breeze. Exhilarated, I danced, skipped, and twirled in the hot sun. Walking back to my car, I called for Haley who had disappeared into the vineyard. She was running like a wild banshee and a man in a Lincoln town car drove by slowly, peering at me through thick dark sunglasses.

"Haley," I yelled.

She was nowhere to be seen.

"Haley girl. Come!" I screamed and gathered the drawing supplies I had set on the stone wall.

She bounced into view, thank God. "Come on. In the car. Good girl," I said as I shut the passenger door.

The man had driven off but now he returned and stopped. He was parked near the end of the road next to the vineyard and I felt frantic all of a sudden, telling myself he wasn't *them*. I threw everything in the car and searched for the auto lock button on the door handle. My mouth was dry. My head was pounding. My hands were tangled in my hair. In an instant, I was a mess.

"It's not them, Michelle. It's not them…"

November 21, 2000

We had been watching TV when the sound of wrenched hinges and tortured wood echoed through the walls. Breea and I spun around in the direction of the thundering crash to see splintered pieces of wood from the back door frame sailing through the air and scattering across the floor. The door flew open, slamming against the solid oak entertainment center just behind it. Three masked men emerged from the darkness and through the door, dressed in black from head to toe. They were holding guns and their heavy black boots pounded loudly across the floor toward Breea and me. *This isn't happening. This isn't real.*

In an instant, our life as we knew it was over, replaced by a new and horrifying reality. Everything was happening in slow-motion frames, one more sickening than the last. I darted my glance to the side to see Breea running towards my bedroom. I tried to get up and follow her when the sharp cold barrels of two handguns pressed into my temples.

"No, No, No!" I screamed as the thinnest man headed for the area where Breea had just disappeared. Grabbing her by her hair near the bathroom adjacent to my bedroom, he dragged her into the living room and shoved her little face to the floor. A large, muscled hand gripped a handful of my hair so hard, I felt it rip away from my scalp. A heavy, thick knee pressed into my back, driving my face into the carpeting. A metallic taste filled my mouth. "*Breea!*" I screamed. She was nowhere to be seen. Visions of rape, torture, and death assaulted me while these three phantoms buzzed around me like a swarm of angry wasps.

"She's all I have," I heard myself saying. "Please don't hurt her. Please. Please."

"Shut up bitch, or we'll pistol whip you in front of your kid!" a voice growled. I smelled his sour stench as I tried to lift my head from the dark brown carpet. The iron hand pressed harder into the back of my neck, while a boot's bulky sole positioned itself in front of my nose. I inhaled vinyl and rubber.

"Are you going to kill my Mommy and me?" I heard my daughter ask in a voice that was more childlike than I'd heard in years. I breathed in a sob of relief and a nose full of snot and carpet fibers. *She's alive! Thank God!* I wanted to look at her, see her eyes, touch her face, and calm her fear. I ached to let her know with a single glance that we would be all right. But I didn't know if that was true.

The man holding me down wouldn't let me pick up my head. I heard someone unrolling and ripping what sounded like tape as I raised my eyes to see four black dog paws, pacing with agitation.

"Voodoo," a raspy voice called out. "Sit!" I had seen the Rottweiler earlier, I thought he was a stray. I was wrong. His name was Voodoo and he was theirs, sent here to intimidate us, to soften us for the kill. I'd fed him and patted his head but he circled me now, breathing heavily, drooling, and panting.

"I'll do anything," I pleaded with the masked strangers, "but please don't hurt my daughter."

"Shut the fuck up before we beat you so bad you never get up!" some one said. "Besides," he added, "no one can hear you scream way out here, you dumb white bitch. Just do what we tell you and no one will get hurt. Did you know we've been watching you get undressed every day for weeks?"

"For *months*, man," added a low voice. "Damn! What I'd like to do to you. Such a fine white ass you got, lady!"

The large man drove his knee harder into my back while he bound my wrists and ankles with duct tape. I strained against the tape but I couldn't move my hands or feet.

"I'd like to give it to you right now," said the man standing near my face. "All those things I saw you do with your boyfriend. You know, the guy with dark hair you had over here a while back. Bitch, you *do* look good walkin' around your house all naked and shit."

I scrunched my eyes tightly closed. When I was as young as Breea, I believed that if I couldn't see my dad hitting my mother, then they couldn't see me.

"Yeah," he went on, "we seen you. You ever had a black man?"

My stomach lurched. Terror overwhelmed me, but I said nothing. I was praying.

"You know you want it," he continued in a sickly sweet voice that made me want to turn his gun back on him and feed him a bullet right down his throat.

"Don't worry, bitch," he said. "We ain't here to rape you. Not tonight. We're not stupid enough to leave DNA at the scene of a dumb white girl's house."

My daughter was in earshot. Did she understand what they were saying to me? I hoped not, as I listened to a pair of footsteps stomping around heavily, heading toward the kitchen, down the hallway, and finally into the northernmost part of the house. I heard the sound of drawers opening in my bedroom. He was looking at my things. I wanted him out of my world. He was touching, and to me tainting my belongings, and making them unclean.

One of the men grabbed my taped wrists and jerked me upwards, spinning me around on the carpet, and burning the skin on my knees. I didn't care because now I could see Breea, lying face down on the floor near where my feet had just been, with silver duct tape on her wrists and ankles. A gun was pointed at her head. "Run, baby, run," I wanted to cry out, but neither of us could do anything. "Are you okay, baby?" was all that would escape from my throat.

"I've stopped shaking, Mommy," she said bravely.

The taller man came out of my bedroom and into the living room, waving around one of my Victoria's Secret red lace thongs. "Let's see you put this on and do your thing right now," he said. His voice was vile.

Shame and fear colored my face. I shuddered with revulsion that strangers were touching my underwear, invading the most intimate parts of my life. These people had been stalking me for months and I'd never seen any of them. How could that be? Was it my fault? Why hadn't I been more alert? I barraged myself with admonitions that I couldn't have kept my daughter safe from these monsters.

Napa, CA July 8, 2001

Haley barked through the window and startled me out of my flashback. I couldn't get those images out of my mind as I shifted my attention to the man in the black Lincoln with tinted windows. Was he following me? Stalking me? How did anyone know I would be here? "No," I told myself. "You're not doing this to yourself. Do not let them win!" With my heart racing, I turned the key ignition, revved the engine and I peeled out of there. I passed the man in the car who seemed to watch my every move until I disappeared from his view, and he from mine.

As the sun rose higher in the sky, a scathing heat came with it. I broke out into a sweat and my car labored until the little black gauge on my dashboard hit the red zone. I pulled over and turned off the engine right away, something my ex-husband, Jeff, had taught me. He had been so good at taking care of our cars. I sat under the shade of a towering eucalyptus tree, fidgeting and looking around almost constantly for the black Lincoln, while the engine cooled. Jeff and I had taken several road trips together between California and Washington State, and while he never stopped to take in any scenery, he'd made me laugh a lot and he was easy on the eyes. Standing almost 6 foot 3, he was as handsome as a movie star and smart as a whip, but underneath it all, he was hiding major insecurities. He and I had turned out to be fundamentally different people with completely opposite goals, but when I met him, I'd been so mesmerized and in love, I'd gotten married too fast to find out whether or not we were compatible.

After about an hour, my car had cooled down enough to give it a nice, long drink. Haley and I got back in and I hit the road feeling strangely capable and in control even after the close encounter with the stranger in the black car. Several hours and a few towns later, I stumbled on a perfect campground overlooking Clear Lake. I was surprised when the woman at the check-in office pointed to a campsite that was the closest one to the water with its chiminea and a straight shot to a dock.

"The sunsets here are spectacular," she said. "Do you have a tent?"

"Well, sort of," I told her. "It's an old Army style tent. One of those things I can't figure out. I think it's broken. I've been sleeping in my car."

"K-Mart is just up the road. They're having a sale. You might want to go get yourself a new tent. I have a tent pad here you can have if you want it."

I wanted to jump out of my skin with joy at the thought of a good night's sleep in a tent with pillows and blankets and a tent pad. "Yes. I'll take it. That would be wonderful. Where's the K-Mart?"

"Straight up this road about two miles. Can't miss it."

I paid cash for the campsite and jumped in my car, ecstatic at the thought of a K-Mart tent score. When I arrived, there were tents on sale for 20% off. The two-man dome tent was on a shelf by itself. There was one left and I grabbed it, paid the cashier, and headed back to the lake.

It took me over an hour to figure out how to set up the colorful shelter. When one of the rods went into the small pocket to hold down one side, the other would slip out. I was in a wrestling match with a two man tent and it was winning. The sun was getting lower in the sky and I finally had it. "Put your right foot here, Michelle," I told myself. "Okay, now put your left hand there and slide the pole through the tie you already made, Now the other side." It was a puzzle, a game of Twister, and eventually, I was victorious! The tent pad fit like a glove and I put down every blanket in the car with pillows propped up. My flashlight was in place, just above the pillows in the small dangling pocket near the mesh tent window in the back. My small blue and white plastic cooler fit near my feet next to the arched zipped door. It was perfect.

I wiggled into my bathing suit inside my tent and called Haley to follow me to the small dock that extended into the lake. My feet swayed as I felt the surface of the water. People were fishing nearby. Sailboats dotted the water while diamond-like rays of sunlight glistened and danced on the lake. It was the first time in as long as I could remember noticing that I was breathing. Actually feeling myself breathing in and out. I stood on the edge of the dock and jumped. Haley was next. Hitting the water was like a baptism. There were no *them* for that moment in time. There was no pain or insecurity or worry or doubt. It was just me and Haley, splashing like teenagers on summer break.

When the sun was setting, I cooked a can of baked beans on open flames, set up my camera on a tripod, and recorded a short video for Breea. Then Haley and I got ready for our first night in our new digs. Haley nudged her nose under the blankets as I listened to children chattering and the crackling of firewood. I zipped up the tent and plopped down like a rag doll, disappearing into the soft cotton blanket, burying my head into the pillow until it all faded to black.

6

SHELTER ME

I waved to the kind woman who gave me the tent pad and inhaled the scent of bacon wafting from the diner on the corner. I wished I could afford a big, hot breakfast. I didn't want to run out of funds so I opted for cereal out of a small, thin cardboard container I could pour milk right into. I had stockpiled several of them for the trip.

I drove towards Northern California past the massive ancient trees in the Redwood Forests. Breea would love them, I thought to myself. I stopped the car and walked across a thick tree stump, balancing my steps, my arms swaying back and forth like a tightrope walker, a smile turning the corners of my mouth upwards. The sensation was unfamiliar since I hadn't smiled like that in a long time. I let the warm feelings fill me up. The little girl inside of me was emerging, curious, and ready to explore, and I was thrilled to greet her after all these years.

The stretches of road were getting longer and more desolate. As I drove further away from Napa and closer to the Oregon border I knew there was no way I could camp that night. It was raining again and it was getting dark. I needed a place that was dry and warm. Dead set against spending the night in the car in the rain, I finally spotted a motel sign that flickered neon red letters that read 'Cozy Rooms.' I slowly approached the reception desk, the look on the bored clerk's face as dreary as the stale, faded orange and yellow lobby.

But when she quoted me $35.00 a night and patted Haley on the head, I paid in cash and took the empty room. It was dated and dim and I was not pleased that it was located at the end of the building, so close to the street. But after sleeping in the car, the bed looked warm and inviting. I locked the door and leaned down to remove Haley's leash. I threw my small bag of toiletries and pajamas and I looked for something to barricade the door. The small wooden table would work. I dragged it across the dark green carpet and wedged it the best I could against the door and under the knob. I sat on the bed and flashed back to the hotel room after the break-in where Breea and I had been curled up in the corner. Every place we went back then felt like a prison. My brother Dave had installed several locks on every window in the place we finally moved into after the trauma happened. I also set traps on the window sills and in the hallway in case anyone tried to get in.

"I can hear them screaming in my head, Mommy," she would say as she put her little hands over her ears trying so hard to block it out or make it stop. She was still wetting her pants and scared to go to the bathroom alone so I held her hand and walked her in there. Every time. I would sit with her and put books in the bathroom for us to read to try to make it not so scary for her. I hoped being with her grandma in Alaska was helping her heal. Helping her forget.

I checked out the bathroom in the motel. A hot bath sounded like heaven. I poured shampoo into the tub to make bubbles and I soaked luxuriously, thinking of Breea. Soon she and I would be together again. I could feel my muscles unwinding, my back relaxing as I lay there in a trance, amazed that I had gotten this far. I needed to be strong, not only for myself but for my daughter. "What kind of role model can I be for her?" I wondered. Had I ever considered my legacy to my daughter? What would it be?

I closed my eyes and thought back to a time when my Mom was going through emotional hell, lying in the hospital after yet another suicide attempt. I'd been sickened by seeing her bloated body, black charcoal running down the side of her face and neck after they'd pumped her stomach. Her eyes looked dead and she seemed to be nothing but an empty shell.

"Mom, you need help," I'd said when she was finally concious. "You need to be in a facility that can help you sort this out." I pleaded with her in front of the hospital as she sat curbside in a wheelchair with a few of my siblings nearby.

"No," she retorted. "I'm fine."

How could anyone think they were fine, five days after a suicide at tempt? She continued, "I'll just go back to work and forget about everything. Just get me back to my apartment."

"But mom..."

"I don't want to talk about it anymore," she'd insisted. "Let's just go."

Did I do or say something wrong? Why was she so angry? As usual, I blamed myself. Several days later we brought her home, but she was destined for more hospital beds and psych facilities in her future giving me more reasons to numb myself with drugs during my teenage years.

Self-destruction was the food I'd devoured for so long, I'd convinced myself that God wanted nothing to do with me any longer. I'd felt like a teenage disgrace back then and before I knew it, I was listening to rock music, popping black beauties, guzzling booze from a bottle, and smoking weed. What had happened to the times when my Mom and I had laughed and danced together in the living room, blasting Elvis, Barry Manilow, and Neil Diamond?

I dipped my head underwater in the tub and began to scrub my scalp. I would get through this and Breea would be proud of me. She would never turn to drugs because I was determined to show her a better way. I got out of the tub, dried off, put on my sweats, and set up the video camera. While my hair dried, I talked about the trip so far, imagining Breea watching the tape with me, pointing to the places on the map her grandma had shown her, as I told her everything about my journey.

Noises outside kept my attention moving like a pinball and my nerves seemed to be on the surface of my skin. Cars kept pulling up near my room which was located close to the main road. My stomach lurched when I heard the tires moving, doors slamming and light coming through the cracks in the curtains. I couldn't sleep so I reached for the remote control and turned on the news.

"In today's news…" I heard the anchorman start to say.

November 23, 2000

I could hear a TV reporter on the screen announcing a fifty thousand dollar reward for information leading to the capture of the criminals in our case. We had been invited to my best friend Kristi's house for Thanksgiving, our first outing since the attack. As we walked in I wasn't sure how to interact. I spent years being outgoing, and social. It was different all of a sudden. I was having trouble processing conversations, fielding questions, and dodging glances.

I ran into her living room to see the screen. My bank employer was of fering the reward. There were shots of our old house, my Jeep, and the yellow taped-off area that was labeled as the crime scene. The gunmen were still at large. This was the first time I was aware of any reward.

I watched for a moment and found myself slowly, involuntarily back ing away from the television, and catching myself before I fell. Kristi led me to the couch to lie down. Breea was in another room; I could hear her childish voice. Amid the sounds of people eating, drinking, and chatting calmly that sounded muted and a million miles away, I sensed that I didn't fit in anywhere anymore as I drifted deeper into post-trauma oblivion. I just couldn't fight it any longer. I was drowning with no idea how to save myself.

I didn't know how to describe the fragments of our destroyed life that they found in the house that was now forensic evidence. I couldn't unsee the masked thugs wearing gloves who had ambushed us. I knew that most criminals leave behind small, sometimes infinitesimal pieces of themselves at a crime scene. We needed to get lucky. Maybe that would help quiet all that was haunting me.

News crews had swarmed our house like vultures after we had called 911 as the crime scene investigators scoured the property for clues. A sketch artist documented where each piece of evidence was found. The first big break was discovered in the dirt surrounding our house, where footprints led to and from the back door. With a storm on the horizon, they had to move quickly to capture the prints before rain destroyed the evidence. The best news was that although the criminals wore gloves, they didn't cover their foot tracks. The most overlooked evidence contained within a crime scene is footwear evidence. A pat tern that reveals scratches or scuffs can act like a fingerprint with very identifiable characteristics.

They poured casting material the consistency of pancake batter into the impressions, hardening into a piece of usable evidence. They had one shot to get it right because a single bubble would render the cast of the impression useless. A matching pair of boots or shoes would be significant evidence linking someone to the crime scene where expert photographers snapped technical shots of the prints.

Pieces of discarded duct tape were strewn throughout the house. They found blonde human hair stuck to them, which proved the traumatic violent experience we had had. With latex-covered hands, the electro static dust print collector shone a special light on the slick tile floors, revealing 13 invaluable prints. After that, they lifted a thin layer of dust on the smooth surface of the bathroom floor. Tweezer-shaped instruments put pieces of evidence in plastic Ziploc baggies. At one point a pair of expert eyes picked up a single black, coarse human hair from behind the driver's seat of my jeep.

The bomb squad gathered around what we were told were dynamite sticks. The thugs said the plan was to remove them when they received the bag stuffed with money. I did my part. They didn't do theirs, at least not the ringleader who kicked me out of my jeep. He left them taped to me, digging into my spine. My roommate had removed them by cutting the duct tape and ripping it as my skin and hair hung on to the sticky adhesive. She had placed them on the retaining wall before we ran to the neighbors for help.

Lastly, they vacuumed the house thoroughly and sorted through the contents, looking for clothing fibers, dog hair, foreign particles, and anything else that would lead them to these bastards. By the sixth day of the investigation, my boss had upped the reward money for any information leading to the criminals. Lastly, they vacuumed the house thoroughly and sorted through the contents, looking for clothing fibers, dog hair, foreign particles, and anything else that would lead them to these bastards. By the sixth day of the investigation, my boss had upped the reward money for any information leading to the criminals, one being a convicted felon, bank robber, and parolee from Atlanta, Georgia. 24/7 surveillance of all the suspects began and during that time, phone records were gathered and a mountain of hard evidence was piling up. Informants and greedy snitches came out of the woodwork with information, ratting out their three buddies who had loose lips and so much pride in their plan, they couldn't keep it to themselves. The investigators now had the real names of those involved and they knew they had "Crips" gang ties. They also knew two of the men were violent criminals with long rap sheets.

On the eighth day, it was determined that one of the dowels of wood used for the fake explosive devices had revealed an astonishing piece of evidence a fingerprint left in the paint. Their first attempt to reveal fingerprints via heating and steaming super glue into a mist that stuck to paint had failed so they tried another rarely used technique, their last hope. Since the print was on a curved surface, it was difficult to capture and process for identification, but the careful application of an epoxy material, smeared on like paste, did the trick. The print was lifted, transferred to a flat surface, and processed for a match.

With a search warrant in hand, the team of investigators organized a simultaneous raid at 7 AM on November 29th. The ring leader and his girlfriend, who was a co-conspirator, were supposedly staying in a room at one of the houses that they descended on with full force. The room was empty. Heading to another house on Avery Street, found a thirteen-year-old "wannabe rapper" named Princess. "What the fuck do you want?" was her greeting. Heading to another house on Avery, they knocked on the door. A thirteen-year-old "wannabe rapper" named Princess answered the door. "What the fuck do you want?" was her greeting.

This damaged creature was living in a garage with two of our attackers and the girlfriend of the ringleader. The floor was strewn with used hypodermic needles, garbage, soiled diapers, and a smell of desperation similar to the worst kind of body odor. The house was a hotbed of evidence. Within days, four police cars surrounded the ringleader and his girlfriend, guns drawn and screaming, "Step out of the car with your hands up" at a stop light not far from the bank location. They surrendered. In the trunk was a goldmine of incriminating evidence; a black duffle bag filled with emptied bank cash wrappers, money straps, my stolen credit cards, and other items belonging to me, black gloves, nylon black pants, and in the glove compartment, a loaded handgun.

Another man was surrounded at the tiny motel in Paris, California, and arrested without incident. He still had some of his portion of the haul with him, but most of it had been spent.

Boot prints that they lifted from our house matched the boots they found in the closet, placing them at the scene. Carefully analyzed for color and chemical compound, the paint matched the spray paint can and paint on the glass found at the Avery house. The dowels were an identical match to the outline on the glass found during the initial raid. Finally, the biggest and most valuable piece of evidence of all, was the fingerprint found embedded in the paint itself on the circular dowel and strategically captured on a piece of tape. It had been left by the impatient maker of the device checking without gloves to see if it had dried completely. It hadn't. The print was that of the man they had just arrested.

The last man, the one they called "Bones," the one who attacked my daughter, had changed his name, obtained a fake ID, and skipped the state. He was on the run and America's Most Wanted was about to be on his tail.

Although the forensic evidence should have fool-proofed the case against the suspects, it didn't. Only a mere fraction of what is pieced together to prosecute criminals ever makes it into the admissible pile of evidence. And although two of those in custody made complete confessions, a shocking defense tactic emerged from the ringleader. He claimed I was the one who planned it all, recruited him in a grocery store, and said that I was having an affair with him.

Now it was up to the FBI to prove him wrong. But first, interrogating and traumatizing me was on the FBI's hit list.

Bright headlights from another car pulling into the motel parking lot hit my eyes. My hands reached up to protect them. The news on the television in the dingy room sounded like scratchy static. I sat up and reached for the remote to shut it off. I needed to tune it all out. The crime. The news. The noise. The FBI. The lies. Breea's screams as I walked away with a gun to my back that morning, not knowing if I would ever see her alive again. Not knowing if I would live another day. My mind kept drifting in and out of deep, dark despair as if two separate forces were battling it out for my attention.

Haley was sprawled out on the bed next to me relishing the queen-size accommodations. I reached for the light switch under the lampshade. I needed to sleep. I needed to get it all out of my head somehow, some way.

PART 2
SOUL WIDE OPEN

You're not just someone I love. You're someone I cherish. You're someone who reminds me that amidst all the haze there is clarity and that no matter what, I am loved. You're the whisper in my dark and my heart and soul need you.

7

BLINDSIDED

I woke up feeling optimistic. Just before I was ready to get back on the road, I smiled into the tape recorder and said, "Let's go see what the day has in store." My mood changed when I returned the key to the front desk and loaded my stuff in the car. My left rear tire was flat. I waited for the old sinking feeling, but it didn't come. At least the tire hadn't blown out on the freeway or a dark road in the middle of nowhere. I grabbed Haley's leash and we headed for the Chevron gas station that was just a block away from the motel.

According to Josh, the handsome guy who worked at the gas station, it was safe to roll my car there. Thank God the street was on a decline be cause hiring a tow truck would have blown my budget. So would a new tire. I was praying hard that it was going to be an easy, cheap fix. As I rolled into the station, Josh, decked out in a blue mechanic's uniform, greeted me. My tire was good as new with just a permanent patch.

"Where are you headed?" he asked as I was being handed my keys. "Up near Anchorage," I said.

"Anchorage!? Alaska?!" he exclaimed with what seemed to be a mix of amusement and disbelief.

"Yeah. My daughter is there and I need to get back to her. Long story."

"Where are you driving from? *That's* a hell of a drive for anyone, let alone a woman and her dog."

"I started in San Diego. I have 9 days to get there before her birthday. I promised I'd be there for that." I told him.

"I was born and raised here. Never been anywhere else really except San Diego. I'd never go back. Too many people." he said with conviction.

"I get it. Believe me. Thanks for your help." I shut my door and drove away. By the time I hit highway 101 on the Oregon coast, I knew there was no chance that I would make it before Breea's birthday unless I cut across the interior of the state to I-5. The coast would take far too long. As I drove, I took in the gorgeous scenery along the 101 and the rugged coastline. I couldn't help but think about the scenario that had just played out. The universe knew I had a nail in my tire and knew it was going to rain. If I had kept driving, my tire would have eventually gone flat and there were long stretches of road with nothing and no one for miles.

It was late, dark, and cold. Even if I'd made it to a campground, set up camp, and made it through the night, my tire would have been flat in the morning in the middle of a campground somewhere without a way to get to a gas station. There was something so much bigger going on here than me or this road trip. I wasn't quite sure what it was yet but this trip was a catalyst for something bigger and I was beginning to tap into it.

The massive rocks and ocean were flying by as I made my way north toward the Canadian border. My stomach was growling and I knew Haley needed to eat and stretch her legs. I spotted a sign with an arrow pointing to a small road to my right with the name of a park. I pulled off the main road and parked near a bench and table next to a river. The birds were singing along with the rush of the river that was the color of emeralds.

There wasn't another soul in sight as I grabbed my cooler, set it on the hard bench seat, and popped off the lid. A banana looked like it had seen better days as I took it out of a zip-lock baggie. I had a little milk left and a tiny box of Frosted Mini-Wheats. There was something about that moment that made me feel like quite the renaissance woman. I was doing this on a budget and I didn't need a 5-star restaurant. This was a more beautiful view than I had ever seen at any restaurant.

I enjoyed every bite I took with my plastic spoon, watching Haley explore. I used to sit and watch Breea and our old dog Charlie play in the front yard of the home the men in black had destroyed. The swing set was still fresh in my mind. The birthday parties and Easter egg hunts. It was my favorite place I had ever lived, up on a hill surrounded by open land with the ocean in the distance. Coyotes howled in the night and neighbors so far away, no one could ever hear us scream. It dawned on me that we were the perfect target.

A car pulled up in the parking lot in the park near me. I could hear it coming to a stop behind me, the engine was still running. I turned to see who was joining us and in an instant, I felt myself being mentally hurled back into the backseat of an unmarked government car.

December 2000

An unmarked government car picked up on a brisk December morning to "review evidence." A man with an open face and an easy-going manner introduced himself. He'd been at our neighbor's house during the hours of ongoing questioning that evening after the incident, but I didn't remember him. He seemed nice enough, his short beard and mustache made him look distinguished and his ready smile was encouraging when he wasn't hurling painful and repetitive questions at me. I always thought the law was on the side of the victim, the innocent one. This guy was supposed to be on *my* side of the law, but when he escorted me into a white-walled room with a few hard-backed chairs and a table, it was clear he had other loyalties.

I looked at the people gathered for my questioning, several whom would be my daily companions when the trial began. They looked like your usual cast of characters from any of the cliche cop shows. The DA, the FBI guy, the obedient assistant, and a couple of detectives who didn't know what a smile was. The meeting had supposedly been called so we could all get to know each other and review evidence. So why did the process feel unnecessarily cold from the moment I walked in? Why did they start bombarding me with probing questions that had absolutely nothing to do with the home invasion attack on my daughter and me, the kidnapping, or the robbery? The questions came faster than I could answer them:

"Tell us whom you have slept with in the last three years."
"What happened to your marriage?"
"Did it break up because of your sex life?"
"Was it because you were a stripper?"
"Did you ever have sex for money?"

"How much money do you have?"

"Did you ever lend money to your lovers?"

"Why did you file for bankruptcy?"

"Why are you doing this?" I yelled. "So what if I bounced a check once or if I took off my clothes a hundred years ago because I had a fucked up childhood and wanted to make easy money using men to get through trade school? Am I the first person to ever file for bankruptcy after a divorce? Why are you doing this to me? Stop it, please...." My voice faded as I dropped my head into my hands.

"We're just doing our job, Michelle," said the officer. "They said you were in on it and we need to . . "

My head shot up. I interrupted. "Who said I was in on it?" I demand ed.

"Two of the suspects."

The walls began to sway. I jumped up, knocking my chair to the floor in my haste, unable to control my outburst. "For you people to insinuate that I would ever have anything to do with harming a single cell of my daughter is insane!" I informed them. "For you to think for one second that I had anything to do with this criminal activity is more than disgusting. If you don't point me in the direction of the bath room, I'll vomit on you right here and now!"

I rushed out of the room and down the hall to the ladies' room. I flew into a stall and dropped to my knees, sobbing and vomiting into the toilet bowl. Sweating profusely, I stood slowly on wobbly legs, pressing my arms against the walls of the stall to steady myself. I wiped my mouth with toilet paper, then with my sleeve, and left the stall to stand in front of the sink.

I looked in the mirror at the only person there who would listen to me. What had happened to the corporate go-getter, the woman who loved her job as an Assistant V.P. and felt proud to have made her life work for herself and her daughter? Just when it seemed like it couldn't possibly get any worse, it had.

I splashed some cold water on my face, wiped it off with a scratchy paper towel, and returned to the "interrogation" room. The system that was supposed to help me was turning on me instead. I looked each of the men and the woman in the eye, my voice slowly rising in pitch and decibel level as I spoke. "If you people think I had something to do with this mess that ruined my life and stole my daughter's childhood from her as she knew it, you're out of your fucking minds! I'm not perfect and, yeah, I may have done some things in my life that I'm not proud of. But I worked my ass off for 13 years to get to where I was in my career. I didn't become a teen runaway statistic. It all took more than you'll ever know. I'm not a criminal and my daughter is my world. This line of questioning is over!"

"Hey, Michelle," one man said. "We believe you. We're on your side. We just have to do this to rule you out."

"Tell me another lie, asshole." I thought to myself. If they were on my side, they sure had a funny way of showing it. On the way back to my hotel room, I wondered if there was any difference between the good guys and the bad guys. They were all starting to blend with their blind siding tactics and asking questions that were none of their business. My list of "people I can trust" was diminishing by the second.

There was not a word spoken on the way back to the hotel where the unmarked car dropped me off. The silence said it all.

July 2001

The people who had pulled into the parking lot of my near the picnic bench where I was enjoying a modest breakfast were revving the engine and began backing out to leave. I was left there alone, wondering who in the world was on my side. That was a shorter list than I could have ever anticipated. I needed to find a way to focus on what was ahead now, not what was behind me. It all kept creeping in, trying to infiltrate every moment. I was doing my best to grasp the lessons, and any clarity I could possibly gain.

The trip wasn't even half over. I was running out of money and running out of time to get to Eagle River, Alaska, by mid-day on July 15th. I was making deals with myself about stopping for photos or coffee or food. I had to cut out most of that. It was time to put the pedal to the metal, haul ass through the rest of Oregon and Washington, and get to Canada by tomorrow.

8

NAKED

I was about to start up the car when a pleasant-looking couple walked over to the window. "Have you ever driven through Valley of Rogue River State Park?" they wanted to know.

That particular park had not been on my itinerary but the next thing I knew I was making my way through a lush green tree-lined road. The winding roads created treetop tunnels with people riding bikes or strolling along, holding hands. I had to stop myself from getting out and taking a million photos of the scenery, the lovers walking, and the views. I drove through wide-eyed and in awe.

Within a few miles, I passed a sign for a rest area up ahead. It was along a river. Haley needed to get out to run and I could use some cold water on my face. When I asked a lady in the restroom about the river and if there was a way to get to it, she told me about a path not too far away. It was within walking distance from the rest stop. There was a trail leading down to a rushing stream and as I began to follow it, I fell on my butt, laughing and bumping my way down. I landed at the edge of a magnificent waterfall beside an old brick wall overgrown with moss and curling vines.

The water looked so clear and inviting, I wished I'd brought a bathing suit with me. But the next moment, my clothes were off and I was splashing around in the water, naked as the day I was born. It was one of the most freeing moments of my life. I had skinny dipped in a pool when I was younger with a boyfriend on a dare to impress him, but I never did it for me alone, because I wanted to feel free. I had always wanted to do exactly that. Just be me.

A sudden realization hit that someone might come down the path and see me so I ran for my clothes on the side of the water and wiggled my damp skin into them the best I could. I picked some beautiful pink flowers to put on my dashboard next to the note that read "I love me Mommy" with at least six colored scribbled hearts below it.

I felt like a new woman as I made a beeline for the Canadian border, but my heart stopped when I saw the sign for the Tacoma Bridge exit, heading toward Seattle. I'd forgotten I'd be driving by the place where Jeff and I had gotten married and how that might affect me emotionally. My ex, Jeff, and I had crossed this bridge together when the Navy relocated him for service in Bremerton. In love and dead broke, we'd settled in the small town of Port Orchard, Washington, where we dug up clams for dinner and used the heat from my blow dryer to keep warm on our mattress on the floor.

Jeff had proposed right after the move while we were standing on the dock, as he'd returned from a two-week trip at sea. A month later I be came Mrs. Jeffrey Ramskill, wearing an inexpensive homemade dress. We exchanged borrowed rings for the ceremony but I didn't care. We lasted seven years, a lot longer than it was healthy. After a while, Jeff's drug use became so prevalent, I couldn't overlook it any longer and could not raise our daughter anywhere near that behavior. Divorce was something I had wanted to avoid, but I couldn't. Sometimes what we want is not meant to be.

The pain hit me as I approached the bridge. I tried to see through the tears that were spilling down my cheeks. I had spent all these years being both Mom and dad, working so hard to have a career and provide for us, I never dealt with the heartbreak that was my failed marriage and the loss of a friendship I cherished.

"What's the matter with me?" I chastised myself. "It's been years. I should be fine." I straightened my back. I'd been too busy making a living, having a career, and being a single Mom to truly feel much of anything about Jeff and how much he hurt me. But I was in my car alone now with nothing blocking my true feelings.

I found a safe spot to pull over on the side of the road. I stopped, grabbed my cell phone, and called Jeff. He picked up the phone right away and I told him everything I needed to say. He made a joke the way he always had before. "What's wrong with you? Don't make me do my Fire Marshall Bill." I tried to laugh. He did his impersonation. "Ah, come on," he teased. "That was good. You gotta admit."

"That *was* good, Bub (the nickname I gave him when we were dating), but I'm hurting and I need to talk to you about something important."

Surprisingly, he didn't hang up. When he heard me blubbering, the woman who'd always been tough, strong, and independent, he knew something was up. "Are you okay? Where are you?" he asked.

"I am looking at the Tacoma Bridge sign," I said.

"I can't believe you made it that far, but if I was driving, we'd be there already." He spoke with irony in his voice, but he was right. If he were driving, there would be no pit stops, streams, or paths! That was Jeff, a no-nonsense kind of guy.

I let out a giggle, despite myself. "I just started thinking about the little white church on base we got married in. I loved the house in Port Or chard and that place in Seabeck Holly so much and you running from those cows." I said." "I'm just reminiscing. We've never talked about how badly the divorce hurt me. I think I need to put this behind me and tell you how I feel."

"You're right," he said to my amazement and relief. "It's time for that. I'm all ears, babe."

We talked for almost an hour, reminiscing about the good times. We laughed about the clams and cases of macaroni and cheese, stealing firewood because we couldn't afford to buy it back then, and shared how we felt about our marriage falling apart. For the first time, I could tell he was sorry for what had happened to us.

Just before we hung up, I said, "I'll always love you, Jeff. I forgive you and I take responsibility for my part too." I can't describe how differently I felt after the talk. When I started driving again, I recognized that this road trip was turning out to be more than getting from point A to point B. Earth Wind & Fire's "Sing a Song" was blasting out of my speakers. I was singing again. This was the road to recovery not just from the horrible crime, but from life, from feeling broken and all the heartaches of lost dreams, and buried pain. It was being replaced with something bigger and better that I didn't fully understand yet. All I knew for sure was that I'd never felt so free from my past. After all this time, I was finding myself and I was savoring it.

I was meeting kindred spirits on the road. I remember talking to my therapist before I left for Alaska. She said, "You need to work on your trust issues, with men specifically." Maybe that was beginning to take shape. I had to trust strangers, men to watch my dog, help me get into my car when I locked myself out, and fix my tire. My camera was a buffer. I could talk to strangers, about my journey and how I was photo graphing and recording it all. I wasn't running from anything anymore. What I was running towards was what mattered as I began to open up.

Route 38 is adorned with simple little houses and cabins along the river. I watched them fly by my window. They reminded me of a simpler life. None of the trappings of "stuff." Life isn't about stuff. It's about our relationship with ourselves, I thought. It is about what's going on in side, not what is being collected on the outside. The simpler life sound ed pretty good right then and so did Vancouver. I was getting closer to the border and tighter on funds. I called Judy to ask if she could hold off cashing the check I gave her for the ticket she had purchased for Breea's flight up there. She agreed to hold it for two more weeks. I just might have enough money in my bank account to make it.

I didn't know how the currency worked in Canada so I pulled off the freeway to grab some quick cash out of the ATM. I sat frozen in my car for what seemed like hours. Going near a bank was a massive trigger for me. I gripped the car door handle in one hand and my ATM card in the other, I got out and started walking towards the bank. With every stride, my chest tightened. I could hear their voices, their demands, in my head.

I could feel the money being shoved into the duffle bag they had instructed me to fill up, or else.

In an instant, before I even got to the ATM, it felt like I left my body, just like I did the day I robbed the bank.

9

FIVE MINUTES

I felt tears trying to push through but I stopped them. The last thing I needed was for my staff to see me crying when I was trying to be invisible. I took a deep breath, kissed the picture of my little girl that was on my desk, and reluctantly put it down. Then I relocated my briefcase strategically near the vault as I made my way to the operations area of the building. This way I could make my move without drawing attention to myself.

Janet, a new teller for the day, a substitute from another branch, approached me. I couldn't tell the new girl that she wouldn't be there for long that day. As soon as I had my daughter safe in my arms, I would be alerting the authorities if I were still alive. Either way, I knew that the bank would be closing for the day to investigate what I was about to do, whether I lived or died. "It's going to be an interesting day," was all I said as I showed her where to keep her lunch and which computer she'd be using. *Bad timing for her*, I thought. *Worse for me.*

In my mind I rehearsed my next move, filling the gym bag with cash. But what if Brinks didn't deliver the usual amount today? I casually checked the mobile vault that we called the "cash cow," where we kept a small amount of cash for the tellers' convenience. There was a pile of hundreds in there and I placed them where I could grab them as we went into the vault. Everything had to run as smoothly as silk since the gunmen had given me five minutes to fill the bag, get out of the bank, and get back to my car. The leader's words echoed in my head, "You better get it all or we'll come back and kill you." I needed to make sure there were no delays or surprises.

I watched the clock. I'd never realized how jerky the minute hand was. It didn't sweep steadily but twitched spastically from one minute into the next. I heard the Brinks truck. Through the front windows, I saw the boxy gray armored truck cross the parking lot and drive to the back of the bank. I glanced at poor, unsuspecting Maria, mother of an infant. I hated that I was about to drag her into my misfortune, but I had no choice. If she did exactly what I asked, there would be no repercussions for her. But if she indicated in any way that something was not right or if she tipped off anyone, we could all die in a heartbeat.

A few minutes later, the Brinks truck retraced its route across the bank parking lot and out into the street. They had made their delivery. This was it!

"Maria," I said as calmly as I could, "can you come with me for a second?" I gestured toward the vault. As she got up to accompany me, I grabbed my briefcase, opened the door to the cash cow, and scooped up the hundreds. Together we entered the vault.

I closed the door and turned to face my employee. "Maria, listen to me and don't say anything," I whispered. I quickly and quietly filled her in, lifting my shirt to show her the dynamite. Her wide eyes told me she wanted to bolt but I impressed upon her that Breea's life lay in the balance. I had her check the mechanism on my back for clues or numbers, but there were none. My captors had done their homework.

Then, as if she suddenly had awakened to what was going on, Maria blurted out, "Oh my God, Michelle, you're robbing the bank."

Oh no . . . The microphone! Did they just hear that? I was frozen for a nano second. Was my angel in a million pieces already? Would I be at moment now? I snapped back into action.

"I only have five minutes," I told her.

A vague sense of shame nagged me as I blankly watched my hand reach for the cash. I stacked bundles of money into the bag. Maria stood be side me, shocked and paralyzed, unable to move. I made her promise not to call the police until I was well away, convincing her they had a scanner that could pick up police calls. At least that was what they'd told me and they were calling the shots. My hand felt like it belonged to someone else as I continued to grab piles of money and filled the bag with the vault contents.

"Go out there and help the customers," I told Maria, "and get ready to close the bank as soon as I call. Then you can alert the police and corporate security. Come on Maria. You can do this. I'll call you as soon as Breea and I are safe."

We walked out of the vault together and locked it behind us. The first thing I heard was an employee yelling, "Michelle, I need your help. This new computer system keeps locking up and...."

"I trust you to take care of it. Call Technical Services," I called back to her as I dragged the heavy bag past a line of customers waiting for a teller. The clock on the wall ticked to 9:01 AM. Someone who knew me tried to chat with me on my way out. "Off to an early meeting?" she said.

"Not exactly," I muttered as I headed for my Jeep. I opened the driver's side door and hurled the gym bag with all my strength over the center console onto the passenger's seat before getting in. The talker still crouched on the floor in the back seat, instructed me to drive to the street next to Domino's Pizza. When we passed a particular cul-de-sac, he pointed and said, "Your Jeep will be right here. Find your way back here to your car after I drop you off and then you drive straight home. No cops until 11:00 A.M. Got it? Now drive into that parking area of those apartments and park in number eleven."

I did as he ordered. "Get out." Butler grabbed the bag of cash, his watery eyes glowing with greed, peering through what I could see now in the light of day were large cutout holes in a black beanie that he used as a mask. "Walk slowly," he said in a low, dark tone. I got out of the Jeep and onto the black tar, stepping backward away from the gunman and my car. He climbed over the center console and into the driver's seat, shoved the shift lever in reverse, and backed out of the stall. He sped away.

I was alone. He had told me he would remove the dynamite when he got the money, but I was still wired to explode. What would happen next? Would they kill me now that they had what they wanted? Were they waiting for me to get into my car again before he detonated the dynamite? Or would they shoot us when I got home? Maybe the other men had already taken Breea. Or murdered her. Images of explosions and my dead child tormented me.

My step sped up as I walked to my car. I couldn't move slowly, no matter how hard I tried. I noticed a strange man, all alone, getting out of one car and into another. He was watching me. Was he assigned to kill me once I was on my own? I darted my head towards the cul-de-sac just in time to see a car speeding away from where my Jeep was supposed to be. It was a copper color, with louvers in the back window and a back end that looked like an old Nissan Z28.

There was my Jeep, the engine running, right where the gunman had said it would be. And I was still alive! I jumped into the car and grabbed a pen. For lack of paper, I jotted down the license plate numbers and descriptions of the car I'd just seen on the vinyl seat. Then I drove home like a race car driver, the dynamite still strapped to my sore back. I gripped the wheel, my daughter's name echoing as I passed the bank, flew up the streets of my neighborhood and to our driveway Breea!

"God, please...please, I beg you, let her be alive!" I mumbled as I rushed to the front door, which had been barricaded with a chair. With in human strength, I pushed my way in and opened my mouth to scream for my daughter. No sound came out until the third try.

"Hello? Hello? Breea!?"

July 10, 2001

"Hi, Mommy." I heard her say on the other end of the line when I answered my phone.

"Where are you now? I have my map ready!"

Her voice was the sweetest sound on earth. I tried to gather my composure and get my hands to stop shaking as I shoved the cash I had just withdrawn from the ATM into my purse.

"I'm almost to Canada. Can you believe that?" I said, trying my best to not let her know I had just walked away from a full-blown PTSD flashback and nearly paralyzing panic attack.

"You're still so far Mommy. Are you sure you're going to be here for my birthday party?"

"I wouldn't miss it for anything. Besides, I have a surprise for you for your birthday and it wouldn't be the same if I gave it to you on any other day. I have to make it!"

"And you promised Mama." She reminded me.

"Yes, I did. I won't let you down. I just won't sweetie. I'll see you in a few days. I miss you so so much."

"I miss you the most," she said.

"I miss you the most too. I love you, angel. Be a good girl for Grand ma."

"Okay. We're going to the movies today. I wish you were here to go with us."

"We'll go to the movies when I get there! Call me later. I want to know all about the movie."

Thinking about the last movie we saw together made me smile. It wasn't too long after the home invasion that I thought we needed to start trying to go out in public again. A music store turned into a bad experience when the cashier recognized me from the news reports. Restaurants were not easy because we were both so frightened by everyone around us. Reminders were everywhere and I thought seeing "Spy Kids" would be a great way to get out and not be surrounded by so many triggers.

We walked into the theater and went to the popcorn counter.

"A little butter on top please," I ordered a small bag of popcorn along with a cold drink and a box of my favorite movie theater snack: Milk Duds.

We walked down the hall through the double doors of the theater. Climbing up towards the top of the stadium-style seats, we shuffled across the floor of an empty row choosing the seats closest to the middle. The drapes were made of thick velvet that covered the walls. I could see the dust particles floating in the light above us where the projector was pointed to the screen from the small room with a window above. The previews were starting as we settled into the fabric folding chairs, resting our drinks in the cup holder between us.

"Excuse me," I heard a man's deep voice say.

"Oh, um yeah. Of course," I replied as I swiveled my knees to the side.

A tall, average-built black man and his son, who was 10 at the most, squeezed by us and sat in the seats right next to Breea and me.

"Mommy, can we move to another seat?" Breea whispered.

I could feel my pulse quickening. I knew why she was asking me the question. She was triggered back to that night, to them.

November 21, 2000

The large man drove his knee harder into my back while he bound my wrists and ankles with duct tape. I strained against the tape but I couldn't move my hands or feet.

"I'd like to give it to you right now," said the man standing near my face. "All those things I saw you do with your boyfriend. You know, the guy with dark hair you had over here a while back."

I scrunched my eyes tightly closed. When I was as young as Breea, I believed that if I couldn't see my dad hitting my mother, then he couldn't see me.

"Yeah," he went on, "we seen you. You ever had a black man?"

My stomach lurched. Terror overwhelmed me, but I said nothing. I was too busy praying.

He continued in a sickly voice that made me, a committed peacemaker, want to turn his gun back on him and feed him a bullet right down his throat.

"Don't worry, bitch," he said. "We ain't here to rape you. We're not stupid enough to leave DNA at the scene of a dumb white girl's house."

Breea was in earshot of it all. They introduced her to a fear she had never known before. Their references, their brutality, was now under our skin and in our cells.

January 2001 Movie Theater, San Diego, CA

"Mommy?" she said as she tugged at my pant leg.

"Can we sit somewhere else? The man next to me scares me."

My girl. My sweet girl. A man and his son were sitting next to us. How much more could we take? We were in a movie theater where we thought there would be no trauma. No fear or worry. That didn't happen. Instead, our nightmare was hitting us square in the face. At that moment I knew one thing for sure. I had the decision to make. As Breea's words echoed, *the man next to me scares me*, I reminded myself that this man and his son were not our attackers. They weren't monsters. They are not them. I knew that what I decided to do at that moment would impact not only me but my daughter, too, possibly shaping her views about race and people of color forever. My decision could change the course of our healing on a level I never even considered.

"Sweetie, why are you scared?" I asked.

"He reminds me of the bad guys' Mama."

"But those bad guys are not here. Not every man or person who looks like them is bad or wants to hurt us. Look around, angel." I gestured to the entire movie theater full of people.

"There are lots of people here. They want to watch Spy Kids just like us. This man is just a dad with his son like I'm a Mommy with my girl, ready to destroy this bag of popcorn!" I reached into the bag and shoved a handful in my mouth, making her giggle just a little.

"Let's stay right here and have fun watching the movie," I said. "Be sides, these are the best seats." I did my best to put a positive spin on the situation and ensure that my daughter didn't think it was okay to judge all people of color, or anyone, because of the actions of a few. I was not going to be the mother to perpetuate that mindset. We would heal. We would get through this one moment at a time. One decision to the next.

When the movie was over, the lights came up. "That was great." the young boy exclaimed to his dad. I looked at Breea. It seemed like she had forgotten about the fear she felt before the movie started. She grabbed my hand and asked if we could get some ice cream. We walked to the car, swinging our arms and hands back and forth. As I looked at her, there was a certainty that came over me. My decisions, how I heal, would shape my daughter's future, and at that moment I knew it. It was so clear to me. My recovery would shape hers.

What I chose to hang onto and let go of would determine her healing path too. I wasn't sure what our future looked like but I understood that it was my job to model recovery in a way that was focused forward, honed in on what we could gain from this experience, and would help us both.

10

HOPE

My plan to reach the Canadian border by dark was overly ambitious. I was close but I couldn't drive for another three hours. My shoulders were aching from long days behind the wheel as I wound my way through forests and in and out of solid rock tunnels with a hint of blue skies. The drive had been spectacular and I could feel myself changing. I was waking up and feeling more alive. I realized I could choose to let them win or I could choose to extract every possible lesson from that horrific experience, my childhood, and even my failed marriage. I could use them to propel me forward. The alternative seemed bleaker with every passing mile. I could stay angry and get stuck there but I didn't want that for me or Breea.

During those long days, sometimes I stopped only long enough to in hale a can of tuna and a few crackers or cereal. That was taking its toll and the bug bites were making me even more uncomfortable. There were campgrounds galore on the map since I was getting into rural areas of the Pacific NorthWest where camping was sure to be in full swing in July.

I quickly set up my tent next to a family with a young daughter named Alana. Randy and Kathy, her parents, were gracious and offered to watch Haley while I organized things. I had made it a habit to look for empty campsites near older couples or families in an attempt to feel safer. It worked. Sort of.

With a fire blazing, my folding beach chair perfectly positioned and my shelter up, I had a moment to fix myself some dinner before calling it a night. When I crawled under my blankets and settled into the qui et, I couldn't stop thinking about the movie theater and the man with his son. What else was this ordeal going to teach me? It never occurred to me that I was going on an emotional treasure hunt, finding out more about myself and the world around me than ever before.

I could hear Alana laughing. I love the sound of it. I wished I could remember more laughter from my childhood. But the noise of seven siblings, mostly arguing and bullying, drowned out a lot of the joy back then. My mother's cry mixed with my dad's egotistical brokenness and violent rages created so much instability, it was difficult to ever feel like my feet were planted on the ground. When I was in early middle school, I discovered a place near a stream that flowed over a huge boulder up a path at the end of our street, Big Rock Road. I would sit next to the stream for hours at a time. I had no idea what meditation was back then but looking back, that's exactly what I was doing. I would listen to the birds, the water, and my thoughts. I would take deep breaths and lay back with my face towards the sky, knees bent and my hands behind my head. It was my sanctuary. My hiding place. My church.

I wanted to create a life for Breea that she didn't need to escape from before those men broke down our doors. I was working 14-hour days in the corporate world in pencil skirts and stilettos. I dropped Breea off early and picked her up late. Breea would do her homework, I made dinner, we played games, she took a bath and I read her a bedtime story. That changed after the home invasion. I sobbed in my car behind some of the other parents in the pick-up line when the school bell rang. It was like the scene in Pinocchio when he realized he was a real boy. I felt like a real Mom at that moment. No more after-school care. No more before-school care. I was there for her in ways I had never been before. The horrific crime had torn a gaping hole in our life, and I made sure to be there for Breea as much as possible. I was on the brink of an awakening to what that gaping hole could teach us. What the gift in it all could be.

Now I was out in the wilderness again. My tent was my sanctuary. The road had become my new home in a way. The crickets were loud and the bright moon cast shadows on the trees. I was finding myself. Finally.

Waking up to Haley's whines to be let out of the tent was becoming the norm. We hit the road by 9:00 am on July 11th ready to cross the Canadian border. The landscape near the Canadian border crossing was a welcome sight. I slowed down and inched toward the "stop here" sign. The land there was beautifully manicured, showcasing the national maple leaf symbol. I knew I had made it as I watched the US and Canadian flags swaying in the breeze. There were seven lanes where we all stopped to show the documents I needed to get through. I was hoping for another stamp on my passport and I crept up closer to the lady standing in uniform at the booth.

"I need your passport and proof of permanent residency please." "Here you go," I said. I handed her my documents.

"How long will you be in Canada?" she asked.

"I'm hoping for just three or four days at the most. It is my daughter's birthday on the 15th and I promised I would be there for the party. I am headed to Eagle River, Alaska, about 40 minutes North of Anchor age."

"You're driving alone to Anchorage?"

"Yes. Unless there is another way to get there that I am not aware of," I said with a little humor.

"Well, if you're planning on going through Vancouver, you might want to change your route. On an easy day, driving 10 hours a day, it will take you five days to get there."

"Is there a better way or a shorter way? I can't miss her birthday. I just can't."

She heard the desperation in my voice. "If you go through Hope, there are more paved roads and less traffic. You might make up some time and not get stuck where there are no towns for long stretches."

She asked me to wait a moment and returned with a free map that would help me navigate my new route. "Here are your documents, your passport, and your permanent residency documents. The map will help you get where you need to be. Is that mace?" she asked as she looked at my keys dangling from the ignition.

"Yes. I keep it on my keychain all the time. Being out here alone, camping mostly, with just my dog can be a little intimidating and scary. Bears, strangers, you know." She had no clue that bears were the least of my worries out here and that the boogeyman was everywhere in my mind since the crime.

"I can't let you take that across the border. You'll have to surrender that. It's against the law to carry it here."

I reluctantly handed over my mace suddenly feeling a bit more vulnerable and thanked her for all of her help and the maps. Instead of traveling northbound on the 99, I was pointed East on Canada Hwy/BC. Hope was just over two hours from the U.S. border. When I arrived I pulled into a nearly deserted campground and paid fifteen dollars for a big spot next to a retired couple from Vancouver Island in a small white RV who I soon discovered was traveling across Canada for the summer. My tent was up in no time. I was getting the hang of this.

They welcomed me and took an immediate liking to Haley, a good sign. We chatted for a while and they invited me to join them for a hot meal in a couple of hours. "We're cooking up some chicken," they said, "and there's more than enough. Why don't you join us?"

"A home-cooked meal would be amazing," I said with a big smile. "When do we eat?"

"How about six?"

"Perfect! I'll see you at the dinner table."

I drove off leaving my tent, cooler, and chair behind to go back and take some pictures of a great old bridge I'd noticed on the way here. I'd spotted a small white oval-shaped trailer parked there on a lush green, grassy lot by the edge of a river. An easel stood nearby with a straw hat hanging over its corner. It looked like a Norman Rockwell moment, an irresistible opportunity to shoot some film.

Haley and I returned to the low wooden bridge and explored the river bank. The water was cool and the air was crisp. I tiptoed across rocks, almost losing my balance a few times, and knelt to take a drink and splash some fresh water on my face. I wasn't the same person who left San Diego. Here I was, out in the middle of nowhere and I felt the freedom of it all. The fear was fading into what felt like a distant memory. I was drinking from a river with my bare hands and eating out of cans and I was happier and more myself than I had been in years.

When I reached the white trailer, I snapped some great photos while I left the car running. But when I was through, it was déjà vu. Haley had hit the lock again and I was staring at her through the window wondering how the hell this was going to pan out. I hadn't heeded the fireman's advice to get an extra key made. Once again, Haley was locked inside but this time, we were in the middle of nowhere with dinner plans back at camp in less than an hour.

Within minutes, a young woman stopped her car and stepped out. I'm sure I looked at least someone frantic and she was probably debating whether or not to stop. For whatever reason she hadn't judged the situation as a disaster waiting to happen and headed directly to me, trusting her intuition.

She was about my age and she was wearing khaki pants, a t-shirt, and hiking shoes. A camera dangled from a strap around her neck. She was naturally pretty, the kind of woman who needed no makeup to radiate beauty. She could see my dog going crazy inside the car, I looked frazzled and wet and with a camera hanging off my shoulder. I explained what had happened.

We both laughed at the irony of the situation and felt like we were kindred spirits.

"My name is Michelle," I said.

"Oh, that's my sister's name. My name is Linda."

"That's my mom's name!" I said.

We were both photographers, dog lovers, and soul-searching travelers. I sensed that she recognized that my heart was full of love and adventure, but could also read the deep sadness in my eyes, my brokenness, and my fear.

"My keys are locked inside my car," I told her. "All the windows are up, and my dog is in there. I just stopped to snap a few shots of that great scene over there by the river." I pointed to the easel. "It caught my eye, too," she said. "I'll go get some help. You can stay here with your dog."

She walked to her car and drove back to the gas station where she had just filled up her car to call a tow truck. By the time she got back, I was pacing and in a panic, worried about Haley locked in the car in the stifling heat. But since she had returned, some of the pressure lifted and I dropped the idea of breaking the window to save the dog. She looked okay even though she was panting a little bit. It wouldn't be much longer.

I'm sure it was no secret that I was dealing with a lot. My car was packed with stuff. I looked like a complete mess and my dog was locked in my car with the engine running. But to Linda, my being out on the road alone with my dog represented strength and resilience to get through whatever I was facing.

"Where are you headed?" Linda asked.

"I'm going to a town north of Anchorage called Eagle River. My daughter is there, and I promised I'd make it by her birthday in a few days. Where are you going?"

"I'm not sure." Linda tilted her head. "I just needed to get away for a while. You know, escape from my life and just think. I'm headed for Montana, but eventually, I need to go back home to Philadelphia."

"I can relate."

"Why Alaska?" she asked

"It's a long story," I told her.

"I'm so impressed, even a little jealous, that you're on this amazing road journey from Cali to Alaska. If only I could take the detour and follow along with you to Alaska. It's at the top of my bucket list."

I learned that she was on a bit of a hiatus too, from a life that I would have never imagined. We each had our paths to follow and mine was north. Hers was south. I looked at her closely. I felt safe.

"My daughter is turning 8 on the 15th." I looked down at my dirt cover shoes and legs covered in bug bites.

She looked at me like she was sure there was more to the story.

I was getting impatient waiting for the tow truck when a lovely middle-aged couple walked up to us. The man had a rounded belly, a sign of a contented life, and he wore a friendly, fatherly grin. The woman, middle-aged with an average build, had woven one hand through his arm. The other held a leash with a small white dog at the end of it.

She smiled and held up a coat hanger in the leash hand. "Need one of these?" she asked.

"How did you know?" I smiled broadly.

"We live across the river," said the man, "and we saw you out here. We figured you just need some help and it looked like you were locked out of your car."

The man slipped the coat hanger into the car door and fished it around. He wiggled it until it caught something, and then pulled. Voila! In seconds the lock popped up. I opened the door, and Haley jumped out, her tail wagging furiously. She bumped noses with the little white dog and took off like a shot for the water's edge, where she waded in up to her knees and drank greedily.

The tow truck pulled up, and I approached the driver, feeling a little guilty that we'd succeeded without him. I explained what had happened, apologized, and thanked him for coming. He shrugged, smiled wryly, and left.

The older couple was already on their way back across the river and I called my thanks. They stopped on the bridge and waved. "Coffee tomorrow morning," called the woman, gesturing toward their house across the river. "Any time after dawn."

I turned to Linda. Without considering my manners, I invited her to join me at the campsite for supper with the people who had invited me. I didn't want her to leave because I had connected with her so strongly. That was unusual for me these days and I was willing to impose on my dinner invitation rather than see her drive off. I prayed that my hosts wouldn't mind. It just seemed like Linda and I still had a lot to talk about.

Dinner had cooled by the time we got back to the campsite. My campmates greeted me with apologies for the lukewarm food, and I apologized for being late.

"What happened?" the woman asked, seeming to be genuinely concerned. "We got worried about you." I looked at her sheepishly. "You won't believe it," I said. "I locked myself out of my car, and this lady stopped to help me. This is Linda. Do you mind if she joins us?"

"Not at all," my host said, "but you'd better hurry unless you want it cold."

We sat down to chicken, sweet corn, and a delightful surprise, red wine. Linda and I devoured everything as we all talked and laughed about the adventures we were each having.

The couple had been traveling for weeks, something they did every summer. Linda described her life as an activist and photojournalist, and I rambled on about my daughter and my travels up the coast, but I steered clear of the actual reason I was living out of my car. We were a happy foursome until the couple went to bed soon after dinner. Linda and I decided to take a walk around the campgrounds.

"You want to know why I'm out here on the road?" I asked as the sound of breaking twigs cracked under my feet.

"Of course. I'm intrigued."

"My daughter and I are relocating after three men kidnapped us and held us hostage for a long time." I paused to breathe and then I carried on. "They threatened to kill us and made me rob the bank I managed. We needed to get away because we felt threatened and scared all the time, and I decided that taking us away from the pain back home was the best thing to do. My daughter is in Alaska with her Grandmother. I took her there a week ago and went back home to get rid of most of our stuff and then drive back to be with her. So here I am, following my inner guidance. It's been a lot." I shared more details about the abduction without looking up. Then I raised my eyes to hers.

"Oh, my God. You're not kidding, are you?" she said. "I wish I was."

"I can't believe you're out here on your own after something like that. That's pretty gutsy."

"Actually," I said, "I never imagined doing this myself, but this is bigger than me, bigger than anything. I feel called to do this if that makes sense. It's been amazing."

"To be out here like this has to be a calling," she said, nodding.

"What about you? What's your story?"

Linda was still considering hitting the road, but we were having such a good time, it was getting dark and I invited her to stay. At that point, after the red wine and the wonderful food, and the connected conversation, we knew she was staying put for the night. My invitation to crash at the campsite was a welcome offer. Rather than setting up another tent we decided to both crash in my tent. We still had a lot more to discuss.

"Well," said Linda, "I've just left Washington state, hiked and camped out in the rainforest in Olympic National Park. I'm on my way to Whitefish Montana to spend some time with a friend and hike the Glacier National Park." It was clear that she was exceptionally kind, and adventurous, and had some deep healing of her own to do.

"It hasn't been long," she continued, "since I returned from an intense and amazing trip overseas and before that Colombia where I had met with survivors of trauma, the war. In Colombia, we went into the jungles to be with a displaced community that had survived a brutal massacre. I needed some serious soul searching to reconcile in my heart and mind what I witnessed there, and to figure out how I can best rally support for these communities."

I was stunned. This woman was a real-life freedom fighter. An activist for people who needed it most around the world. My long days of researching victims' laws popped up in my mind as Linda talked about her journey as an activist. She'd been on the front lines, taking a stand for what she believed was right. I knew I was headed in that direction, too, focusing on the healing aspect of surviving trauma, but when and how remained a mystery.

We continued the conversation in the tent and shared countless other stories. She helped me process a lot of thoughts, especially about what my next moves would be when I returned to California someday after the trial. I shared with her that it was suggested that I change my name. After giving her a few options that I had scribbled on a napkin on the flight home before packing up my SUV and driving out of dodge, I mentioned my middle name, Renee.

Linda got excited and told me that Renee was her birth name, but her parents changed it to Linda at the hospital because the nurse confused Renee with Ronnie (her mom had a thick French accent). It was an epiphany. I decided to use Renee as my new last name right then and there.

We talked late into the night and when we tried to get some sleep, we couldn't because the trains were running regularly, whistling their warning signal as they passed the campsite. Morning came and we headed for coffee with the sweet couple that rescued my dog from the car. We walked along some trails up to a waterfall near their home, both of us clicking and twisting our cameras to capture the moment from every possible angle.

We parted ways after we exchanged music, contact info, and the knowledge that the universe had brought us together. I needed her in my life at that exact moment in time, and she needed a renewed sense of goodness in others. We both needed that. We bolstered one another and gave each other a gift that has no price tag or expiration date. We had not only an incredible memory but a friendship that we knew would continue to last a lifetime. Our meeting wasn't coincidental by any means. It was one of shared dreams, sorrow, love, and even rebirth, offering us both a renewed sense of optimism that tomorrow would be a better day than yesterday and that we all can make a significant difference in the lives of others.

It *was becoming obvious* that this journey was a wake-up call, a reminder that there is more to life than we realize when we're buried in work and deadlines and don't take the time for the things that matter. Real connections. Understanding. Compassion. Love.

It was my dream to help others heal from violent trauma. It was her dream to bring awareness to the violent traumas that were occurring everywhere and tearing innocent lives apart like ours were. At that moment we knew miracles are not only possible, but we can attract them to us. It may have taken a bit of blind trust and faith to heed my distress call, and for me to go with my gut and invite her back to my campsite, but we knew we were destined to meet, and not so ironically, in a place called 'Hope'.

11

CROSSING BRIDGES

The weather report said it was going to drop to 8 degrees that night in Quesnel, Canada, a cute, quaint town 1700 miles from where I needed to be. I could only sleep a few hours a night now. I had to make up time if I was going to get to Breea's party. I found a sweet campsite near a lake, got myself set up, and stripped off my clothes before I eased my way into the water.

There was something about my naked body being submerged in the cold water that fed my soul. Nothing between my skin and the life force that is nature, water. Being completely vulnerable, letting go of all inhibitions, and being unapologetically in the moment was an absolute high. I was drunk on the feeling of being out in nature, capable, strong, in control, and hell-bent on getting to Eagle River.

I wrapped my wet hair in a towel and wrapped my body up in a white ¾ length robe that I had dug out of the back of my SUV. It felt like I was at a spa. I looked the part except for my bare feet touching raw, uneven dirt. I passed out early and tore down my tent three hours later before getting back on the road. It had been forever since I had any resemblance to a real breakfast and when the scent of bacon and eggs hit my nostrils, I pulled into the small restaurant parking lot and ran in for a hot breakfast.

"Can I have two eggs with bacon, please?" I said to the man at the counter.

While I was waiting for my order, I took a gander at the music selection on the wobbly, white cassette tape rack near the register. There weren't too many songs that stood out to me but when I spotted Timepieces: The Best of Eric Clapton and Bob Segar and the Silver Bullet Bands Stranger In Town collection of smash hits, I felt torn. I couldn't afford them both. I couldn't afford the one I was going to splurge on or the breakfast that was waiting for me at the counter.

I counted my money. Things were not looking good. But I had been on the road for days, much of it without a radio signal, and the same old tapes playing over and over. I was ready for something new so I could groove and jam down the open road. I paid the man behind the counter and left the store knowing I made a good choice.

Haley was chomping at the bit when I got back in the car with two pieces of bacon.

"One for you. One for me." I said as I fed her a thick cut of fried pork.

I'd never tasted such sweet bacon and savory eggs. I inhaled them. They were melting in my mouth as I tried to chew slowly enough to make them last a few minutes longer. After Haley licked the paper plate, I ditched it in the trashcan and headed towards the canyon route, with the wild, rugged, and sparsely populated Yukon territory up ahead, singing along to "I shot the Sheriff."

The black bear in the middle of the road didn't flinch as I whizzed by him. The mountains were enormous with jagged peaks and white caps. Rivers were raging and roadside waterfalls were everywhere. Immovable, massive gray rocks and stones resembled a source of strength and stability on the road, much like the obstacles I had overcome. I gazed out over the land. They resembled my journey of overcoming struggle after struggle and were the epitome of what it meant to endure change, storms, heat...life. Maybe that's why I'd been drawn to them at such an early age. It was a refreshing new perspective.

Historic buildings, bridges, and tunnels helped the time pass by and kept my boredom and anxiety at bay. Stretching out my legs after six straight hours of driving in a small town founded by gold rush settlers back in 1859 south of the Yukon, was a perfect place to grab an ice cream cone. I took in the history of this quaint gem I had stumbled upon and wandered as my eyes looked through antique shop windows.

Fatigue was setting in. I had to muster up a way to make it at least a few more hours since the days were so long in this part of the world this time of year. It had been strange setting up my tent while the sun was still up in the sky knowing I could have made it another hour. But the clock would read 10:00 p.m. My brain was trying to adjust to this strange new phenomenon.

The old town was pretty dead and rolled up by the time we left and it was only 5:00 p.m. I had a ton of light left and stretching woke me up enough to get in some miles with the hope of making it to Prince George by the time I was too exhausted to go on. I was hauling ass praying I didn't get stopped for speeding. My calculations put me behind by a few hours so I sped up my pace and hoped for the best.

When I pulled into the next campground, it was a larger one than I'd seen so far. The gravel road led to all of the campsites twisted and turned like it was its own neighborhood. This place was in the sticks. A thick, dense forested area had a lake in the center of it. I drove what seemed like far too long, looking for other campers. They were all so spread out. That was probably great for them but my safety zone included families or older couples near me so I could sleep better at night, knowing I had people in earshot.

It seemed appropriate that Whitney Houston was belting out "One Moment In Time" while I made my way through the massive campground looking for a spot to call home for a few hours. I was supposed to check in with someone at some point but I was trying to decide if I felt safe enough to stay there. I passed a silver oversize van on my right and wasn't ready to give up. Finally, I spotted an open campsite right on the water. I pulled up and put my car in park. After a quick assessment, I realized someone must have just left. The fire pit was still warm and had a dying flame and one tiny log that I was sure I could get going again. I gathered some kindling and blew on the coals until a flame ignited and caught the kindling on fire. I didn't want to leave to go find whomever I was supposed to check in with. I didn't want to lose this perfect place, perched just above the water with an unobstructed view of the lake. If they came to discover me there, I would check in then and pay what I needed to pay. I lucked out and was begging God to not let us get kicked out. For now, I wasn't leaving and whipped my tent into the perfect position to see out to the water the moment I opened my eyes the next morning.

There was a private little path that led straight to the water. It was only a matter of time before I would be in it. With a new can of bug spray in hand, I doused myself and turned to look for Haley.

"Haley," I yelled. "Haley girl!" I kept calling her. She was nowhere in sight.

The campground was so spread out, I had no idea which way to go to look for her. I jogged down the gravel road, screaming her name over and over. 15 minutes later I heard a man's voice.

"Are you looking for your dog?"

"Yes, white and brown pit bull." I walked in the direction of his voice.

The man was camping with his girlfriend in the large silver van I had passed earlier. Haley looked guilty as sin as I walked up to thank them for keeping her there.

"I'm so sorry. She broke her leash a few campsites back." I tried to explain.

"No problem. She's beautiful. Where are you headed?"

Everyone seemed to ask me that question. "Anchorage," I told them, not wanting to explain that it was Eagle River just north of Anchorage.

"Oh wow. You know the roads are unpaved on the way there. Are you sure you can make it?" I could see the doubt on his face. I was getting used to it. Almost everyone I had met on the road, except Linda, didn't think I was going to make it.

"I've heard. But I'm good. I have a reason to make it there no matter what." I told them as I thought to myself, I am the queen of no matter what. "Thank you," I said.

"You're welcome, and good luck," he said as I tried to hold Haley by her collar and walk back to our campsite.

Feeling like a Marlboro woman, I cranked open a can of Irish Beef Stew and plopped it on the metal grates above the flames of my campfire. I was in for a cold night and gathered up my thermal underwear and a thick jacket. The sun was setting on the lake and I had to get a few hours of rest. I shared my can of delicious stew with Haley and climbed into the comfort of my perfect little slice of heaven.

I was startled awake by kids riding their bikes down the dirt path just beyond my tent. It was early, but later than I had hoped to get started. I needed a jolt of something to wake me up after my deep sleep. I knew the lake was frigid. I didn't care. It was exactly what I needed. I eased my way into the water and eventually fully submerged myself. Holy crap, it was cold. Now I knew how those people who participated in an annual ice plunge felt. I tried to get Haley to come with me. She wasn't having it.

Alert and rested, we set out to conquer the mountains of the Canadian Rockies. I could not have been more in the moment than when I was driving up through the mountains, towering peaks on both sides of me, and Eric Clapton's "Wonderful Tonight" lyrics pouring out of my radio. I hadn't felt so purely, deeply in the moment, and connected, ever in my life.

"She puts on her makeup and brushes her long blond hair. And then she asks me, do I look all right? and I say, darling, you look wonderful tonight." And

then that guitar lick. *So good!* I thought to myself. My window was down. I'd been behind a man on a motorcycle for miles and miles now and began to wonder about his story. On the road, you begin to wonder about everyone's story. We all had one. We all had a reason for being out here with our hands and hair in the wind racking up the miles and the songs that took us to places that only music can.

The air was so fragrant, it was as if I were in a flower garden, filling up my senses. With every deep breath, I was getting closer to understanding my purpose for this trip. The purpose of my life. I was beside myself cruising on a two-lane road, the sounds of the music and the growl of Harley Davidson in front of me mixed with unforgettably green, lush scenery.

The road was getting rougher and more narrow. I could tell I was climbing and there could be something to see on the other side of the hill. I was right. There was definitely something on the other side. I stopped in the dirt on the side of the road just over the hill, watching several young boys jumping off of a bridge into the water below. I clutched at my stomach for a quick second when I recalled having a vision of jumping off a bridge to my death in the few weeks that followed the crime, landing in the deep waters below. It had been one of my suicide visions and although I didn't want to hurt myself or die, I struggled to find any other solution to shut off the noise in my head. I called my brother Dave at one point and told him about my suicidal thoughts, and how the knives in the kitchens were calling my name, promising freedom from all the emotional pain I was in.

As the boys took turns jumping and applauding each other, I thought about Breea. How would she feel if I'd gone ahead with my plans to end my life, and she had to watch my corpse being hauled out of the water? What on earth had I been thinking? Thank God I'd learned in my therapy sessions that I could replace negative thoughts or images with new ones. The therapist had taught me how to retrain my mind and this was a perfect opportunity to test the theory.

I thought about my siblings too as I sat there watching the boys in complete awe of their innocence and un-jaded sense of wonderment. Was I ever like that? I wondered what my brothers would do now if they were there with me. As kids, my siblings and I would go to a place in Santee, Ca, called, of all names, Butthole Rock. It was a giant rock with a crack right down the middle that looked like a big, fat ass crack. Hence the nickname. We would climb to the top, and pick mistletoe from the trees to sell door to door. I remembered how we were scrappy hustlers from a very early age. But the most fun was when we would jump from the top of Butthole Rock into the river below. It wasn't as high as the bridge I was looking at, but it was high enough to pause each time before I leaped.

I watched the boys take turns jumping from the bridge, applauding each other, swimming to the rugged river's edge, and starting all over again. I turned off the ignition, stepped out, and introduced myself to one of the young boys, a chubby kid who was too mortified and shy to take off his shirt and jump in. I tried to get him to go for it with me, but he refused. "If I can do it, so can you," I urged him.

He was dead set against it. Although he was friendly and encouraging when I told him I wanted to jump with his group of boys, I could see that his self-esteem was suffering.

"I bet you'd make a great cameraman," I said, offering him the camera. "I may never get this chance again and I'm documenting my whole trip from San Diego to Alaska."

He nodded enthusiastically. "Are you a movie person?" he asked.

"No," I said, "just a lady who needs to remember what it's like to be a kid again."

I stood on the edge of the bridge holding hands with a bunch of boys. They couldn't believe a woman in her thirties was about to jump with them. "You sure you wanna do this, lady?" one of them asked.

"Yup. I'm positive."

Together we all counted, "One, two, three," and we leaped into the air. My fear evaporated mid-jump and I hit the freezing water, screaming with joy while the boys screamed right along with me. It was astounding that the moment I jumped, it was as if my negative visions and past suicidal thoughts flew away with the wind. I was having a ball and I climbed back up on the bridge to do it again. "Raceya to the top," I said.

"You are too cool," one of them said as we clambered back up the bank for another leap. "I wish my Mom was like you."

I hadn't heard the word "mom" in days. Breea would be proud of me. I was proud of myself. I wished I could call her and tell her what just happened, but my cell phone had stopped working after I crossed the border.

I thanked the boys and when I got back in my car, they waved frantically and screamed, "Good-bye, good-bye." I hoped that I taught them that you're never too old to be a kid again. This road trip was teaching me that growing up means facing your fears, your past, and your dreams head-on.

12

ROADSIDE CAFE

Two hours later I was closer to the Yukon Territory and staring out at a black, ominous sky up ahead. I knew I was headed into a heavy-duty storm. I came upon a small church with a white steeple and I stopped to take some pictures, of course. Suddenly it started to rain and a handsome man on a cross-country ten-speed bike rode up and stopped about fifty feet from my car. I'd passed him a little ways back and noticed his good looks and muscular legs. His bike was packed like a miner's mule with a bedroll and minimal camping gear.

"Hello," he said as he pulled out his camera and started snapping photos of the same old white and blue structure.

I jumped in my car trying hard not to think about him. A few miles up the road on the left-hand side, I could make out a sign that read "OPEN" on the door. It was a small coffee shop with an old wooden door that creaked and slammed shut after you entered. An overweight, sweet-faced woman greeted me as I shook myself off. Haley was in the car curled up with a blanket. This was my chance to have a hot cup of coffee or a bowl of soup and wait out the storm. I looked outside. It was torrential.

Through the sideways sheet of the downpour, the man on the bike came into view. He was pulling up out front and trying to get his bike up the stairs to prop under the awning to keep it and his things as dry as possible.

"I have a small table over by the window for you Miss." The woman said and gestured to the two-person table near the window to my right.

"Oh. Great. That's great." I tore my eyes away from the man outside.

Within minutes he entered the coffee shop, pulled his head hear off, and wiped his drenched face. He looked around for an empty spot to sit out the storm. The table in front of mine was open. He sat and ordered a cup of black coffee and asked to see a menu. When he looked up and saw me sitting in front of him, I could tell he recognized me from the old church.

"Oh hey. I just saw you a few miles back at the church."

"Yep. You did."

"Great old church wasn't it?"

"Gorgeous. Glad we got a few shots in before this mess hit. It's coming down. How long do you think this is going to last?"

"No clue. Looks like it is going to be a while though. Mind if I join you?

I looked into his face to see if I could trust him.

"My name is Tony," he said.

Tony was an Englishman on a three-month bicycling tour across Canada and Alaska, before heading back home to the eastern part of the United States.

The rain was beating a rhythm on the roof of the café. Several more people rushed inside to escape the downpour, and in a few minutes, we found ourselves helping the only waitress there, pouring fresh coffee for customers escaping the wrath of the storm. We were having a great time, laughing and acting like we owned the place.

"This is kind of fun," I said to Tony as we passed each other holding coffee pots.

"Kinda? I'm having a blast!" He smiled ear-to-ear. I was stunned at how breathtakingly attractive he looked.

"More coffee, sir?" I joked and flirted with him.

"Why, certainly."

The woman with the ponytail came up to us. "You two are great," she said. "I wish all my customers were so nice. Here's your soup. It's on the house."

When the rain finally stopped, Tony asked me to spend the rest of the day, and night, with him.

"Come camp with me. We can keep this fun going. I'll make some gourmet rice and keep my hands to myself. Promise!" he teased and gave me a glance that made my vagina feel things it hadn't felt in months.

I wanted to say yes. God, how I wanted to say yes.

Every bell and whistle was going off in my head. Was he a good guy? A serial killer? A good kisser? A rapist or was this the stars aligning? My mind was racing and tapping into old familiar territory. Manipulating and getting what I wanted from men was an unhealthy relationship with sex and self-esteem that began as far back as I could remember.

Growing up, my dad often called women whores. I didn't know what that meant at the time, but soon it was a name directed my way and when I did figure out what it meant, I figured I must be one if my dad said so. Watching him grab my mother's face hard and push her up against the cabinets in the kitchen, throw her body down the stairs, and tend to her bruising and battered body was only half of it. The verbal attacks were vicious. The first man I ever loved, and desperately wanted to love me, was an abuser of the worst kind.

As I grew older my looks, whether I realized it at the time or not, became something about me that my dad found acceptable. His friends at the car dealership would greet me when he took me to visit them, introducing me like I was some sort of trophy. I was incredibly uncomfortable not knowing what to say as I reached my hand out.

"Nice to meet you," I said, looking down at my shoes.

My dad's hand would reach for my face and grab my chin, shaking it slightly back and forth. "Look at that face. Isn't she gorgeous?"

"She's a looker all right." I'd hear them say.

There was something about the way he wrapped his arm around my neck like I was one of the good ole boys. He would chat with them for a while, ask me to sit in a few brand-new cars to see how they felt, tell me I looked good in a fancy car and then we would leave without buying anything. We couldn't. We barely made rent half the time and spent days and weeks sometimes without electricity, water, and barely any food.

By the time I was in high school getting the attention of boys, I ended up falling for a guy named Victor. He had long blonde hair, and beautiful blue eyes, he was wearing a rock-n-roll t-shirt, Colorado boots, and a chain hanging from his wallet to his jeans. Victor wasn't in the best crowd but I didn't care. I fell into his trap and pretty soon, I was smoking weed, popping pills and acid, eating mushrooms, and dabbling with cocaine. He was dabbling with meth, something I tried only a few times, and loathed how it made me feel. I didn't care for how any of it made me feel, but it was better than feeling the agony and reality of my home life.

Just before I turned sixteen, I climbed out of my bedroom window one night, ran softly across the wood-beamed patio covering, and jumped down to the earth to freedom. I ran straight into the arms of my first boyfriend, but my illusions were quickly dispelled by his sudden bursts of jealousy and anger. The abuse started not long after I lost my virginity to him at his house where he lived with his Mom who let him turn the garage into the local hang-out, party spot.

We started selling drugs out of the garage and within months, I discovered I was pregnant. I knew I wasn't ready to be a mom. I was high, lost, beaten down, and marred. I knew about abortions, the physical aspect, but I didn't know about the emotional toll it would take on me. When I walked out after having my unborn child sucked from my uterus, I was a shell of the 16-year-old girl I thought I would grow up to be.

Victor's abuse became more frequent and more violent. Friends at a party came into the bathroom once to drag me out after hearing him beat me and pull me by my hair when he imagined I was flirting with another guy. I had to escape, but how? That was when and how tapping into the power of manipulating men with sex began.

One of his best friends had a wild crush on me. He was tall, stalky, dark-haired, soft-spoken, and handsome. I liked him, maybe even loved him in some way, but I was too damaged and scarred to truly know how to love anyone, including myself. He was my way out. I knew Victor would never mess with Jason, no matter what. I sold a few bags of drugs and scraped some off the top to sell on the down low, risky, but I had no other option at the time. I took the extra money from selling the scraps to go buy a new outfit and showed up and Jason's door ready to do what I had to in order to protect myself and get away from Victor. It worked. Sort of. We had a few run-ins at parties, one including a crossbow being pointed at my head, but eventually, he moved on to his next target.

When it was safe to leave Jason, I did. My ability to manipulate men and hurt them before they hurt me was cemented by the time I was 17. Soon, I got a job at Burger King to pay rent on a single room, and I decided to take an ROP class to become a Certified Nurse's Aide. I moved up from a fast food cashier to a waitress across the street, just catty corner from Burger King. I eventually took on a few caregiving jobs so I could ditch my life serving coffee, pancakes, and eggs at Bob's Big Boy in the morning while scrubbing office building toilets by night. Life was not about a cap and gown for me. It was about survival and when my dad showed up with the cops at my high school, I dropped out during my senior year, only 3 credits shy of earning my high school diploma.

I started going rock to concerts with my friends, wearing makeup and teasing my hair in a semi-wild, vixen fashion. Soon enough, we were spending time backstage with groupies, and hanging out with famous rock stars. After being handed backstage passes by a man who appeared from behind the stage after seeing us in the front row, we were invited to join the band on the bus. We scurried in our mini skirts with our badges of honor through the crowded lines of onlookers. They were waiting for just a glimpse of the band as they dashed from the San Diego Sports Arena to their Motorcoach.

Soon we were on the tour bus, laughing, and partying with members of Iron Maiden, all but Bruce Dickerson. He was tucked away in the back of the bus in his 'suite' most of the time. When they asked us to head out on tour with them, we were *IN*. It was a once-in-a-lifetime opportunity. We threw my friend's car keys to my brother out of the bus window. We swore we would call from wherever it was we were going, and drove off with the band and enough cocaine to get us through the next few days.

We would trade VIP passes for weed when we ran out and hoovered cocaine multiple times a day and into the night. We played in hotel pools, with band members and crew, met opening acts like Twisted Sister, went shopping to get more clothes, and felt like we were *almost famous.* The high didn't last and, although I was asked to stay, the band kicked my friend off the tour in Vegas after catching her stealing from the room in the back of the bus. I couldn't leave her there alone nor continue on by myself. We called a friend to come to pick us up in Vegas and headed for the City of Lost Angels.

The Hollywood party scene at the Roxy, the Rainbow, and the Hollywood Palladium were my stomping grounds. I had become the very thing my father had accused me of being, long before I knew what the word "slut" meant.

It wasn't long before I became ennui with the emptiness of that lifestyle and when the bus driver from our tour with Iron Maiden asked me to join him to go pick up the up-and-coming band, Bon Jovi, on the east coast,

I declined and soon walked away from drugs after a night of heavy booze and LSD.

I sat on the couch in the far left corner at the party and took a hard look around me at the people and the environment I was in. I listened to the screaming message in my soul that told me I didn't belong there. It was telling me to get out. Right now! I left the party in the middle of the night and made my way to Pacific Beach where after several nights living homeless, I found a "room for rent" sign and sweet-talked the young man named Bob into letting me slide on the rent for the first two weeks until I could get a paycheck under my belt.

I decided to fall back on the Certified Nurses Aide training I had completed as part of an ROP course in High school. I was elbows deep in bedpans and dressing bedsores. I found myself getting far too emotionally involved with each patient, the majority of whom were elderly, paraplegic, or quadriplegic. I cared too much, felt too much, and I could not detach. One particular guy was different. He was a middle-aged, high-functioning paraplegic named Jim. This man would twist his legs crisscrossed, then walk on his hands since his legs didn't work. One afternoon I discovered a collection of pornographic photos as I was cleaning out the room below deck. I asked him about them. He informed me that he had an exotic dancer business where men would hire *his girls* for parties. When he introduced me to Jeanette, a gorgeous red-haired stripper, her stories of glitz, seduction, and financial independence got my attention. I wanted that for myself, but could I do what Jeanette did? I decided to find out.

She brought me with her to a private bachelor party late one night to begin my training. I watched and learned. What was so bad about showing off your breasts to a group of men who paid you money to strut around and act enticing? This was my chance to get back at men, manipulate them and take their money without ever giving them anything in return except a shot of my tits? By the end of the night, when the men cheered and cajoled me to get up and show them what I had, I strutted to the music as 25 men chanted my name and threw money at me. Not only did I make my entire month's rent money in one night, I also took center stage and got the male attention that temporarily filled the void I'd felt in relationships with men my entire life.

That feeling of power was heady stuff and I learned to dance in a sexy way that drove men crazy, and even incorporated a bit of routine with a long string of pearls that left them begging for more. This was a new high with a new job that paid hundreds of dollars for two to four hours of what I considered flirting. That was a lot more than I'd ever earned and soon, it was "goodbye" to nursing and "hello" to the world of exotic dancing. I would sunbathe by day and dance topless by night. The best part was being on stage, under the lights, staring right into their souls. When the music began to play, I'd escape into it as the rush took over and I could be someone other than Michelle.

I used my feminine wiles, and damaged self-esteem, to my full advantage. I hid my lack of confidence behind heavy makeup and short skirts. The highs were fabulous, but I ended up feeling weary and disappointed in a life that I had initially labeled "glamorous." What was glamorous about topless dancing, getting back at my father, or getting through some sort of trade school to support a family I didn't have? I ran with a crowd in which we understood each other and we didn't judge. But unlike some of the other girls, I had my limits.

One night, Jeanette drove me to a multi-million dollar mansion on the cliffs above the sea, where she was living with her boyfriend. They offered me a large room with an ocean view, all the house privileges I wanted, an invitation to a very swanky, exclusive "OUI" party in Beverly Hills, and no rent.

The catch?

I would give them fifty percent of the money I earned being a highclass call girl. I have to admit that I considered it. They made it sound so wonderful, with high-powered type clients and outrageous money, but being a hooker, even under the guise of another title, was taking it too far. I told them I'd think about it and an hour or so later, we took a drive to discuss the possibilities. The sun was just setting as we pulled into a gas station and the same voice that told me to run from the party that night, was nagging me again, telling me to run again as fast as I could. I jumped out of the car and ran while they were in the mini-mart, buying Diet Coke.

I walked to the corner and stood there. They drove the car beside me and rolled down the window. "Come on, Michelle," they urged. "We love you, you know that. Get back in the car."

I'd heard that one before. I wasn't falling for it even for a second. I knew I had to get away from them. When they saw that I'd made up my mind, they idled a moment and then drove away. There I stood in my mini-skirt and a very tight tee shirt, lost, battered, and alone...again.

I arrived back at the room I was renting and buried my face in the bottom bunk of the bed. My roommate, Bob, came in and asked if I was all right. I told him I wasn't, explained what had happened and he, with his crazy curly blond hair and warm embrace, let me know it would all be okay. I continue to dance for a living, to pay for training for my next chosen profession Dental Assistant. Dancing could provide me with the money I needed to pay for schooling, and as soon as I could manage it, I would quit.

The voice that had guided me away from the party house and away from the woman and her boyfriend and becoming a "call girl" was back. It was that same voice that told me to go back to San Diego and get rid of most of my things and drive back to be with Breea in Alaska. That voice was telling me not to go into the woods to spend the night with the handsome, sweet man traveling on his bike across Canada with whom I had just spent only a few hours at a roadside cafe to escape the storm.

It was barely sprinkling by now and he was persistent. I felt the old familiar tug to want to fill the internal voids in my life with sex and attention from men. I wanted to rock his world and say yes to allowing him to rock mine. But there it was. That voice telling me to say goodbye and get back on the road to go be in my daughters' arms, not his. He was standing close. I could feel the electricity. I stroked his thin riding shirt. I could feel his chiseled stomach underneath it. I was aching for a man's touch. I glanced up at the man named Tony.

"I have somewhere I have to be," I said. "It's just not in the cards. I'm sorry. I have to get back on the road."

I turned my camera around and pointed it at him. I wasn't sure how it would turn out. I didn't look through the viewfinder. I just pointed and took the shot. He smiled and walked towards his bike. My old self was kicking in. But I had decided to change all of that and I did not give in.

This was my chance to start fresh, make new choices, and pay attention to a new code of self-love. I'd found out the hard way that "just one night" could ruin my life.

I shoved down my fantasies of what Tony had in mind, how he looked naked, and everything else about him. Rather, I cherished my newfound self-respect and sense of safety. Nothing was worth losing it again, but I had to admit, it felt good to look across the table at a man once again, instead of crossing the street to avoid him. He was gorgeous, he had treated me nicely and he knew how to laugh and make the best of things. But I didn't *know* him. It wasn't safe, I decided. I declined his offer and said goodbye.

My mind argued with my impulses for miles. I hadn't been in the company of a handsome man for an eternity, it seemed. I craved to be held and kissed and loved. "Go back and surprise him," an inner voice urged me. "You can't pass up an opportunity like this one. How often do they come around? It's just for one night. Nothing has to happen. And if it does, so what? You'll never see him again." My therapist had told me to work on my trust issues with men. I think I made some progress in the coffee shop that day. But this wasn't really about trusting him at all. It was about trusting myself, and my intuition and following it no matter what my body was craving or how I was feeling.

Tony mounted his bike, clicked his shoes into the pedals, and disappeared. I was closing the gap between me and my daughter with the rugged Northern Yukon Territory just up ahead.

13

RUNNING ON EMPTY

I was back on the road at 6:00 a.m. The night before had not been kind. The rain returned, this time accompanied by strong winds that were pulling my car to one side as I gripped the wheel. I was entering the part of the country that had fewer paved roads and more gravel and dirt than I expected. As my SUV bumped and shook, I was dodging deer and moose that appeared seemingly out of nowhere. There were flying pieces of gravel and potholes left and right. I knew there was going to be no campsite tonight. Searching every possible turn-off, rest area, or nook in the road, I finally landed in a spot on the side of the road. I reclined as much as I could and shut my eyes listening to the wind whipping across the open road, causing my car to shake.

It was freezing and I couldn't get close enough to Haley in the passenger seat to suck up some of her body heat. It was impossible to get comfortable. I wiggled, put my steering wheel up as high as I could get it, tossed and turned, and let out some deep, hard sighs. "This sucks!" I screamed as I fought the urge to pound my fists on the steering wheel. But what good would that do? I was in a foreign land in the middle of the night, shivering, without another soul in sight. My eyes glanced at the back seat. I remembered the attacker being crouched in the back seat of my jeep, still in his black ski mask with cut-out eye holes and a gun pointed at me as I drove towards the bank.

Now I was a million miles away from home, or what used to be home. I was a million miles away from the bank, the investigation, and the harsh stares. A million miles away from the top of that hill looking down over all they had destroyed. A million miles away from the women who told me to "pretend it never happened."

November 26, 2000

I stared in disbelief at the bony counselor, dwarfed by her large pink cushy chair in her plush carpeted office. It had been five days since the crime and Breea and I were hoping she could help us.

"Pretend your door was made of steel," she said, "and they couldn't break it down." She leaned toward me and smiled nervously. Her mousy dark hair was severely pulled back into a bun at the nape of her neck. Her thin lips matched the tiny arches of eyebrows she'd painted above her dark brown eyes. "You see?" she said smiling again without involving her face, "just pretend it never happened." She performed a flourishing gesture with her hands.

"But it did happen, Mommy," Breea said softly. She was sitting on the carpet on the other side of the office, playing with a Lego set.

"Yes, baby, it did," I said defiantly, wondering how this woman managed to get a license to counsel anyone. I needed a qualified trauma therapist, not a family and marriage counselor five days after the crime. I had needed someone at the scene, but that didn't happen, and since then our trauma was compounding daily. It seemed that Breea and I were suffering a variety of symptoms that neither of us could control or understand. We thought we were being followed most of the time, we both suffered constant stomach aches and Breea insisted on riding on the floor instead of the seat of the car. I'd hidden behind bushes more than once during those days. I'd even run out of Safeway one afternoon, leaving my groceries behind, certain I'd spotted one of our attackers in one of the aisles, wearing his ugly mask.

The worst part was that previously normal sounds now jangled my nerves. Loud television shows and the crashing of garbage trucks early in the mornings strained my nervous system beyond belief. This woman disguised as a counselor had no idea what we were going through. I took Breea's hand and we left, both of us crying together back to our latest hotel room. By the time Dave, my brother, showed up at the hotel, we were emotionally destroyed, unable to make decisions or take any sort of action.

The day before, my boss, Brad, had given me his corporate credit card to cover any expenses related to the crime while we were at the hotel they were paying for. By day five, though, he started broaching the "back to work" topic. I knew the pressure wasn't coming from Brad himself. He was getting heat from his superiors which was obvious from his sensitive voice and struggle to discuss it with me. From a bottom-line business perspective, I understood. They wanted their results-oriented Bank Manager back. I wanted to tell Brad that I would return to work when I could get into the car without trembling or imagining a masked gunman in the back seat or when I stopped awakening every night from gruesome nightmares.

I relived the trauma over and over again in scrupulous detail. I could feel the dynamite sticking into my back and smell the leather boots under my nose and hear the duct tape ripping. I had many fearful dreams like this one I wrote in my journal:

I'm walking down the street and snakes begin to appear lots of them surrounding me until I can't move. Suddenly I'm grabbed by my feet and taken to a strange house against my will. I'm kept there for days with other girls also being held. I can't get away because of the snakes and barbed wire.

I try to flag down a sheriff. Then I find a phone and try to call my mom. I'm crying uncontrollably, asking her why I'm being held for ransom. The energy is frantic, as I search for a way out past the snakes. Inside the house, there are no doors in the filthy bathrooms. I awaken crying, begging for a way out of the place where I seem to be trapped forever.

When I told Dave my dream, he insisted that both Breea and I get a massage to help us sleep. This, I agreed, would be a great way to immediately deal with the negativity now attached to anyone touching us. It was the first time I had even the slightest thought about how to heal. The masseuse was a kindly woman who helped get some of the kinks out of our sleep-deprived bodies. The relief, however, was momentary, transient, and fragile. The same demons arrived with dusk and so did the noises and agitation that would not allow me to drop into sorely needed slumber.

Dave began speaking to my boss for me. I simply could not cope with my mounting stress and I gained a new appreciation of my brother's emotional depth and his capacity for empathy. I kept imagining my car insurance being canceled, which it was, and telling the lien-holder to come to tow my Jeep away. I couldn't drive it anymore with a ghost in the backseat, and I didn't care what it might do to my credit. I wanted it gone.

My fears escalated thinking about whether or not I would ever be able to work again, and that I would never be normal again. I just couldn't fathom how life would ever get better with no career, no home, no car, no nothing. One afternoon, my father showed up at the hotel with a bouquet of flowers. It may have been a heartfelt gesture but his unexpected visit triggered a resurgence of my turbulent childhood. He'd been so angry for most of my life, he reminded me of the men who had kept me hostage. Though, I owed him a big thank-you. If he hadn't been so selfish and abusive while I was growing up, I never would have known how to handle the gunmen the way I had. Being my father's daughter had taught me how to deal with others' selfish behavior since he had trained me to walk on eggshells and avoid breakage the technique I used with my kidnappers.

I remembered that once my father traded in the family car for a three-wheeler motorcycle that revved loudly enough to satisfy his insatiable ego. When he had extra cash, Dad bought an expensive leather jacket to enhance his image while we walked around in our second-hand clothes. On rainy days, I was devastated that Dad made us wear green plastic trash bags with holes cut for our heads and arms, as he drove us around town, showing off on his "I'm so cool" machine.

I didn't trust him back then and I still didn't trust him when he tried to say something to comfort me. I'd wanted to hear those words all my life, and now it was too late. I was too wounded to care as I listened with half an ear. I questioned his motives concerning the visit, wanting to believe it was all about love. But I suspected he liked the chaos, the hoopla, and the press that would single him out as my father. His visit caused me so much stress, I was relieved when he left, praying he would not return.

I was not relieved, however, when my brother Dave left. I understood he had to return to his life with his son, Shawn, in Los Angeles, but I was forlorn without him. I watched him drive away late one evening, leaving me to face the dark shadows climbing over the balcony. No matter how many people told me differently, I could not shake the belief that someone somewhere was lying in wait to attack us. Poor little Breea had spoken barely a word in days and we held onto each other tightly each night, stripping the bed, piling up linens to sleep on the floor between the bed and the wall of the hotel room so we would be completely out of sight from the monsters trying to find us. I rocked her to sleep, unsuccessfully trying to sleep beside her, afraid to lose my tenuous grip on both of our lives.

I made the following journal entry at 4:00 AM:

December 10, 2000

I miss my life before they took it away. Breea is getting worse. Scared of doors and windows now. She said she could hear 100 doors slamming in her head last night. When will it end? I see THEM on the balcony, climbing over, scaring me. I better go to bed and hold Breea. I wish we weren't alone.

The ringing telephone jolted me awake early one morning. I jumped up to answer it, finding the concierge at the other end of the line. We were checking out that day and he wanted to know what time we'd be leaving. I'd found an apartment-style hotel in which I could cook our meals. It was located near the beach, a familiar place that Dave and my old roommate Kim, and her sister, thought would be a good spot for us to begin to heal. It seemed like just the place, so we moved in.

I had a small kitchen where I could cook and we could take walks on the crowded streets. But my plan to re-introduce myself to the world at large again backfired. One afternoon, when I went to the local Music Warehouse to buy some music, a clerk saw my name on my credit card.

"You're the one from that bank robbery, aren't you?" he said. "You're staying here at the Carlsbad Inn, right? That's such a trip, what happened to you?"

I grabbed my credit card and ran out of the store, leaving the CDs behind. If this guy knew who I was and where I was staying, the criminals could find us in a second. I rushed back to the inn, locked the sliding doors, and stared into the mirror. "Why?" I asked myself. There were no answers.

I threw off all my clothes and stared at the puffy dark circles beneath my eyes. Permanent lines on my forehead had popped up overnight, aging me well beyond my years. I didn't recognize myself. All I could see was a frightened woman, stripped naked, both inside and out, struggling to stay conscious.

The next day, the prosecution team asked me to return to the old house to relive the worst experience of my life, this time with cameras rolling. I phoned Dave, unable to face reentering the scene of my terror without my brother. He drove in from Los Angeles, picked me up at my hotel I was trembling when we drove up the driveway for the first time since our ordeal. The FBI agents were already there and a wave of sadness swept over me as I looked out at the view. I saw ghosts of happier times in the front yard for BBQs, Easter egg hunts, and pushing Breea on the old swing set. These things tormented me as I walked along the front yard. I braced myself as I entered the empty house, but nothing could have prepared me for the nuclear blast of agony that hit me in the stomach. I stumbled from room to empty room. Dave stood by me, struggling to keep his composure as I became more and more agitated reliving our pain and suffering.

When I got to the bedroom where they'd forced Breea into the closet, I lost control. I staggered at the doorway and grabbed onto the jamb to steady myself.

"Are you all right, Michelle?" Dave asked. "Can you do this?" I nodded.

"Are you sure? We can come back."

I was sure. I wanted to get this over with so I could leave and never return to the memories. It was all still there the men on the sofa, their dog, the smell of marijuana, the pounding rap music locked in my memory, frozen in time, re-living itself over and over. The watery, bulging eyes, the guns in my temples, Breea begging me not to leave. I suddenly rushed from the house and flew into the car. I'd had enough. The house on the hill was haunted and my flashbacks were taking control of what was left of me.

After nine nearly sleepless nights (I think I dozed for about an hour each night), the attempts of my friends and family to get me to socialize were proving unsuccessful. Kristi tried renting a funny movie, one with Rene Zellweger called Nurse Betty. We popped popcorn and pretended it was a regular home movie night. But I shrank into the couch when a scene showed Ms. Zellweger with duct tape around her wrists and ankles. It was still too real for me.

By the time the FBI arrived to escort Breea and me to Children's Hospital's Chadwick Center for the videotaping of her testimony, I felt mistrust. It only got worse when I had to wait outside while they took my traumatized daughter into a private room with a therapist I'd never met. They not only kept me out. They also refused to allow me to watch Breea through the two-way mirror adjoining the room.

I crouched in the hallway, feeling helpless, hunched over at the waist, and curled up. A woman with reddish hair and a kind face approached me, wanting to know if I needed help as I sat crouched with my back up against the wall of the hallway. When I couldn't answer, she took me into an office and invited me to sit on a comfortable leather chair. I was scratching my skin, passing my fingers roughly through my hair, and rocking from side to side, unable to speak.

The woman went into her nearby office and picked up the phone. "She needs help," she told someone on the other end of the line. She asked them to bring me a pill for anxiety. Then she knelt in front of me and softly said, "Tell me what happened to you."

So there *were* angels among the monsters. I sobbed. "I don't know," I said. "I don't know what happened to me. I don't know what's happening to me now. It's all a big mess and I don't know what to do. Everyone keeps taking her away from me. Everything is gone...everything is gone..."

The angelic woman gently repeated her request to tell her what happened. I tried to control my hands from kneading my hair as I started to speak about the crime to someone without judgment for the first time. She made a follow-up call for the anti-anxiety medication.

"Can you get someone down here with crime victim paperwork too?" she said. "No, no one has helped her in nine days. I know it's ridiculous. She and her little daughter are the victims of a heinous crime. Do you know the story of the bank manager from the news? Yeah, well that's them. Bring the minor forms as well. Thank you."

I knew with certainty I could trust this woman. She wanted me to feel better and although my hell was still alive and well, suddenly I was not alone. I took the pill she handed me, waiting for a half hour until the medication began to soothe me. Within an hour, I was calmer than I'd been in days, but the skinny man the FBI called "Bones," was still at large.

As Christmas vacation approached, I dreaded the season that had always been my favorite, especially since Breea was born. I used to shake jingle bells, throw rocks on the roof to sound like the reindeer's hooves and I always set up a camera to capture Breea's joy when she ran from her bedroom to the tree to see the gifts wrapped in colorful paper with great big bows. Our tradition was that after she saw the tree on Christmas Eve, she went back to bed and waited for morning to open her gifts. But this year, it took everything I had to face Christmas and the celebrations that accompanied it. I was certain that the crime couldn't steal the spirit of Christmas from us, but I was wrong.

Once again, it was Dave to the rescue. He and his thirteen-year-old son Shawn took Breea and me to the local Christmas tree lot. Breea loved Shawn, a long and lanky blonde-haired blue-eyed kid four years older than she. We got a small tree which we smuggled into our latest hotel room and we decorated it with a few drugstore ornaments. We placed small white lights over it and hung stockings on the wall with pushpins, determined we would have Christmas this year as usual, despite the way we both felt.

On Christmas Eve, Dave and Shawn joined us as I put the presents under the tree and set up the camera just like in years past. When everything was ready, Dave shook the jingle bells and we waited for Breea to run out from the hotel bedroom but she didn't come. He and I looked at each other sadly as he shook the bells again. Still no Breea.

I went into her room to find her hiding under the covers of the bed we shared, shaking, crying, and holding her stomach. When I asked her to come out and see what Santa had left her, she wailed, "It isn't Santa. It's the bad guys coming to get us."

My broken heart broke all over again. My daughter was afraid of Santa Claus. I gently talked her down and she followed me into the living room, clinging tightly to my leg, hiding behind my nightgown. She looked at the tree, at Dave, at Shawn, and at me. "I just want to sleep, Mommy." She ran back into the bedroom and dove under the covers.

After one more sleepless night, I was running on empty. Christmas morning came, we unwrapped our gifts, emptied the stockings, and headed to Kristi's for our traditional gift exchange with her family. By then I felt like a zombie, going through the motions with no sleep. *Where is the joy?* I wondered as I watched Breea clutching her new doll to her chest far too tightly. Kristi gave me a bound journal to write in instead of the random pieces of paper I would grab or rip from Breea's *Winnie the Pooh* notebook. It was the perfect gift for me, but that night, Breea was holding her stomach again, feeling sick and wanting only to sleep. I sobbed for her and me, realizing just how much had been stripped from our lives. Would we ever feel safe again? I feared we wouldn't, but one thing was for sure. It was going to take a village to get us even close.

14

DUST AND GRAVEL

A speeding car that seemed a bit too close spit dirt and gravel onto my hood, rattling my car and jolting my attention. I had no idea what time it was and found my keys in the center console. After a quick trip to walk Haley and pee in the bushes, we were back on the road trying to make up some more time. I couldn't resist a hot shower at a rest area just up the way and found a power source in the bathroom to charge my camera. I tried to forget about the memories and flashbacks that had plagued me the night before.

A man in a nearby coffee shop gave me a cup of hot, sweet caffeine. It lightened my mood. He was the human equivalent of Eeyore. The way he stood. How slowly he moved and when I said, ``Have a good day!" it sounded exactly like Eeyore when he uttered under his breath, "You too."

There was a beautiful body of water to my left and mountains to my right. 40 miles away, I discovered, were well-known natural hot springs and if there was something I needed to make a pit stop for, it was a relaxing dip in a hot spring to ease the stiffness in my body from so many hours behind the wheel.

The long wooden walkway that wound through lush green foliage to the natural hot springs heightened my level of excitement and anticipation. I could see the steam rising in the air before I reached the end of the path. As I stepped onto the deck surrounding the hot water that was wreaking of sulfur, I saw at least a dozen people in the water and near the shower preparing to jump in. I stripped off my clothes, fastened my bathing suit, rinsed in the cool shower, and inched my way down the steps into the deep, hot water that bubbled up from the earth.

The people were welcoming and kind, taking pictures of me in the springs so I could have them to share with Breea. When they asked me where I was headed, I told them about my journey from San Diego and my final destination is a town near Anchorage.

"You're driving alone through the Yukon and Alaska? That is crazy. You know a lot of the roads aren't paved, right?" they warned.

Here we go again. None of them believed I was going to make it. They chuckled when I told them I had two days to get there and they wished me good luck. I didn't care what anyone said. I was going to make it. I had a lot of people to prove wrong at this point and in a way, it gave me even more energy, motivation, and determination than I already had. All I saw for miles and miles were unmarked, unpaved roads. Construction zones came and went and trucks not being mindful of anyone else on the road flew by pitching rocks onto my windshield until one finally cracked it right in the middle. When trucks weren't passing me by, slow-moving RVs were slowing me down and creating a dust storm that I could barely see the road through. What I could see were blue skies up ahead as I drove over a one-lane bridge marked by two wooden tracks that I had to keep my tires on perfectly to avoid getting stuck.

Anchorage was 1040 miles out. Eric Clapton was on repeat when I officially entered the Northern Yukon Territory. I stopped quickly to check out the Sign Post Forest and wrote my and Haley's names, dates, and "San Diego to Anchorage" on a white empty spot on an old faded sign before driving towards the majestic Alaskan mountains.

July 15th Journal Entry

Breea's party starts at 3 pm and I promised to be there. With only twenty dollars left and 3/4 of a tank of gas, I may not make it. But I swear if I have to beg for the money, I'll be there for my daughter. I feel like I've let her down because we don't have a permanent home, but I'm going to change that as soon as I can.

By noon I was completely broke and running on fumes, literally. I blazed through the Yukon like a runaway train. The little voice that had gotten me on this road in the first place whispered, "Go to a church."

I laughed out loud. *Where am I going to find a church?*

I turned the corner and there stood a small white stone community church in Glennallen, AK. I blinked a few times to make sure I wasn't hallucinating. I'd heard about mirages in the desert and I wondered if I was imagining this because I wanted it so much. Then it dawned on me that it was Sunday. The parking lot was nearly full and I pulled into one of the few empty spots.

I walked to the front door of the church, grasped the handle on the heavy wooden church door, and opened it.

"Hello, young lady. What can I do for you?" A pastor greeted me.

I heard music coming from behind two doors leading to the main part of the church. I stumbled over my words a little until I got up the nerve to ask for a handout. Then I inhaled and told the pastor why I was there.

"I've been on the road for days, and I need to get to my daughter in Anchorage by 3:00 p.m. for her birthday party. She turns eight today. She and I were attacked by masked gunmen and left our home to come to Alaska to heal. I've made it this far but I ran out of money and now I'm almost out of gas. So here I am."

He must have thought I was nuts, but he looked at me with a gentleness I can't describe. He touched my shoulder and said, "I'll be right back."

I stepped inside the church and sat in a pew next to an old man with twinkling eyes. I was singing with the congregation when the pastor tapped me on the shoulder and motioned for me to follow. I did and met a man who was waiting in the foyer.

"This is Dave," said the pastor. "I think he can get you exactly what you need. God bless you, young lady, and good luck."

"Thank you so much." I was on the verge of tears.

"Follow me," said Dave. "Sounds like you need a full tank of gas, pretty lady."

I followed Dave to a nearby gas station where he filled my gas tank and paid for it. I cried with joy at his kindness, thanked him profusely, and drove for the next four hours without stopping.

Amid bears, glaciers, and rushing rapids that you only see in magazines, all I could see was Breea. I rolled up into the driveway honking my horn to let her know I was there, exhausted and exhilarated at the same time. Suddenly she was running toward me, Her laughter washed over me and her hugs reached into my heart as she ran out of the door, down the stairs, and into my arms. She was screaming, "Mommy! Mommy!" The citrus smell of her hair intoxicated me as I picked her up and swung her around, both of us squeezing tightly.

"I was afraid you wouldn't make it, Mommy," she said, swiping at the tears of joy running down my face. The family and a few of Breea's new friends from the neighborhood watched us, with colorful party hats perched on their heads.

"We made a pinky promise," I reminded her. "Mommy, I'm just opening my last present."

"No, you're not," I said. "Your last present is in the car."

After I gave her the new fold-up bright yellow scooter and enjoyed some cake, I watched her blow out the candles and make a silent wish. We played a few games, retreated to our room at Judy's house, and drew the blackout curtains. Climbing into a soft, plush bed after tucking her in felt like a dream. Together we said our prayers, spoke of our gratitude and sang "Somewhere over the Rainbow," our special version that I'd sung to her since the day she was born.

Somewhere over the rainbow Way up high, Mommy loves little Breea And sings her a lullaby.

Then we shared her last birthday gift a snuggle. With Breea's little legs wrapped around mine, we fell into dreamland in each other's arms, safe and sound.

PART 3
LAND OF THE MIDNIGHT SUN

We have grown up. We have fallen. We have survived. We've been lost and found again. We have hurt and helped one another, cried and laughed, clung to and let go. Through it all I just want you to know that I never want any of us to give up on any of us. Ever.

15

EAGLE RIVER

Time and places like Alaska can heal invisible wounds in the most fascinating way. We were told we had three months until the criminal trial of our attackers started back in San Diego. I naively believed we would be back home by September. That meant we had the summer to explore the Alaskan frontier and continue healing through the connection to Nature and keeping distance between us and the place where our life as we knew it was torn to shreds. Breea and I took advantage of every moment, not knowing it would be a full year before the justice system could get its shit together. Breea had to start school in Alaska and the small mountain town elementary school was perfect for her. So was her teacher, Ms. Reizer.

"We're new to Alaska," I told her in a private meeting, "and Breea and I are recent violent crime victims. She needs a little more nurturing than usual and she has trouble using the bathroom by herself."

Ms. Reizer smiled reassuringly at me. "Come in tomorrow morning with Breea at 7:45," she said. "Everything will be fine."

The next morning at 7:45 we sat with Breea's new teacher at a small round table inside the classroom. "Hi Breea," she said. "Your Mom told me some stuff that happened to you back in San Diego. Would you like to talk about it a little?"

"Well," she said, looking first at me and then at Ms. Reizer, "three guys came into our house and taped us up and scared me so badly."

"And now you are here and safe, right?" asked the teacher.

"Right," Breea said in a lively tone.

Ms. Reizer spoke slowly and calmly. "What I want you to know," she said, "is that you don't have to be embarrassed about what happened to you. It's okay to ask if a buddy can go with you to the bathroom or to tell me when you feel sick because you're remembering things that happened. It's always okay for you to talk to me. I'm a safe person for you to come to for help. By the way, lots of the kids are brand new because their parents are in the military and they move a lot. They're a little nervous too, just like you. I bet you will make friends fast, though, because you're nice and funny and smart. Okay, sweetie?"

"Okay," Breea said easily. She looked relaxed.

Breea quickly found comfort at her new school and she told stories about her new friends, seemingly putting life back in California further and further to the back of her mind.

Finally at ease with Breea's situation, I used every ounce of my strength to focus on being in Alaska, not San Diego. I had dropped out of high school as a senior after the cops came to take me out of class to reunite me with my parents. The school was my haven until then. I went home and ran away again knowing school was no longer an option if I wanted to stay as far away as possible from the violence, depression, and toxic environment that I had grown up in.

Here I was in Alaska, of all places, healing and waiting for trial proceedings to begin with a lot of time on my hands. What better time to pursue a lifelong dream, than to get my General Education Diploma (GED)? One of my life's greatest disappointments was not graduating. I daydreamed of a cap and gown, holding a degree in my hand one day. Not that I needed it to be successful. My work ethic, drive, and determination was already taking care of that. But I wanted to look better on paper when I applied for my next job, whatever it would be.

I'd believed that I was living up to my potential, that I was intelligent, and that my future was filled with countless possibilities. I could hide under my business suit and no one would ever guess by looking at me that my past was tainted with shame, ugliness, and pain. I'd climbed up the ladder of Corporate America using grit, intellect, and instincts. But each time I'd had to fill out an application for work, I was aware of my lack of higher education.

I decided to be fully qualified in the future, since returning to the banking industry was out of the question. Looking my daughter in the eyes and telling her I was returning to the place that had been the reason for all of our pain and trauma was never going to happen. How could I ever go into a vault again without a full-blown melt-down, flashbacks included? I knew the answer.

So, at age thirty-five, just like my daughter, I was a student again. I passed all my tests with flying colors. I had to laugh that although I'd had success in the world of numbers, my math scores were the lowest of all. It was a good thing that my banking job was more about customer service and relationships and less about number crunching or I'd never have made it past bank teller school. Now, after some focused studying and passing all my tests, I got to put on the blue cap and gown and have my picture taken with my diploma in hand.

I was thrilled when I applied to the University of Alaska, Anchorage, and was accepted. Now I had to figure out what to major in and my mother-in-law was the perfect person to bounce off some ideas

"Try something you love honey," she counseled. "You like to take pictures and write. You're outgoing and I think working with people would be great for you."

I thought for a moment about what I really loved to do. "Photography would work," I agreed, "but it's so competitive and I'm already in my thirties. I love to write and I like public speaking. "Maybe politics or law..."

"Sweetie," Judy interrupted me, "the trial isn't even here yet. You don't know what it will be like and how it will affect you."

"You're right," I said. "Those jobs still hit too close to home for me. Maybe marketing or advertising, something I've already done in banking that can carry over."

"That sounds perfect for you," Judy said.

This tiny woman who stood five feet tall and weighed about a hundred pounds, soaking wet, was the kindest, sweetest person I ever knew. She generally sounded like the voice of reason to me, and we stayed close despite the divorce. With Judy and Breea cheering me on, I made a decision. I signed up for my major in Mass Media Communications with an emphasis on Public Relations.

The first day I walked into the classroom, the stadium seating I'd seen only on television overwhelmed me. I was in COLLEGE, one of only a few students in our thirties, surrounded by a bunch of younger kids who had no idea why they were there. Although I knew that youth was a challenge in itself, I have to admit I felt somewhat resentful as I found the drivel of my younger fellow students annoying.

I made fast friends with my Professor, however, a wonderful intelligent quick-witted woman who became one of my greatest cheerleaders. I was so enthralled with my critical writing class and learning all about American media, that sometimes I forgot about the looming shadow of the upcoming trial. It was so comforting being in the wide open spaces of the last frontier, with regular phone sessions with my therapist back in San Diego. I had a newfound excitement about my place on the campus scene and I was beginning to blossom into someone I had never known Michelle Renee.

July 30, 2001 Journal Entry

Since arriving back in Alaska, I've seen a bald eagle soaring, a giant moose feeding at the side of the road, and a red fox scurrying by with freshly caught prey hanging from his mouth. Snow white mountain goats gracefully climb impossibly vertical rocks and icebergs shimmer blue in the ocean while the glaciers are too vast and numerous to name. I have heard rushing waters with salmon fighting their way upstream with strength and determination. The most impressive sight of all is Breea's smile and the way she sleeps through the night, untroubled.

There we were in the vast Alaskan wilderness. Sitting at a small roadside café after lunch one day, I asked Breea, "Want to go on an adventure?"

"Sure Mommy," she said. "Where?"

"Well, I'm not sure Honey. Let's head North and see where we end up."
"That sounds fun. Just you and me, Mommy?"

"Yup, just you and me."

We drove to Mt. McKinley and decided to stay in a rustic cabin, reminiscent of the cabins of the gold rush era in Alaskan history. There was no water, no lights, no nothing, and we had a blast. We shopped, we ate and we climbed as high as we could. We stood on what felt like the top of the world, taking it all in together, just like we used to. As autumn turned into winter, the snowfall settled upon us, a thick white blanket covering the earth, disguising the ice underneath. We hiked up glaciers and explored ice caves. We strolled along paths that led to incredible waterfalls.

When winter arrived, the brutal cold and unrelenting darkness of the long Alaskan winter felt safe and cozy. I focused on the beauty of undisturbed nature and my newfound freedom from fear. I'd take the cold with its sparkling snows and a clear view of the Northern Lights any day if Breea and I could continue to fall asleep at night with peace in our hearts.

Thanksgiving was approaching when I got a surprise letter from my mom. She wanted to come for a visit but I was reluctant. My Mom had been distant during the entire kidnapping ordeal and its aftermath and I didn't know why. Ultimately, I agreed to let Mom come and be with us. I was glad I did because, from the moment she arrived, it was obvious she needed a rest, just as I had. I made her comfortable. She was on the top of a list I had compiled of "people I needed to forgive and ask for their forgiveness." I felt this was crucial to my healing process, showing Breea what is possible when it comes to moving forward without anger, and sticking to my commitment to have healthier relationships and better boundaries.

After Mom slept off her journey, we reminisced and laughed together. She talked to me openly and honestly about her past for the first time, ever. We cried copious tears of regret, love, and grief. Finally, I could understand as she filled me in on things I never knew about my mom, the young Linda Rea Howard. I was rapt by her stories, able to appreciate a side of her I'd never known existed.

"I will never have another love like Bill," my Mom said of her forbidden relationship with the father of my oldest sister, a married man twice her age. "I wasn't ashamed about the affair or having his baby. Everyone else had a problem with it and then, your dad came along at the right time, I guess. He was handsome and said all the right things. But by the time I realized he was battling some powerful demons and blind rages, I was trapped. It was too late. I never really recovered from his beatings."

It was a whole new experience for my Mom to confront her past, and admit her mistakes as we became closer and found common ground. There was so much more to talk about, and so many questions about my childhood.

My throat closed up and I couldn't speak. I grabbed her and hugged her hard. My eyes filled up and I couldn't say a word. The whole family had become numb over the years. We didn't talk about all that we had survived. We swept it under the rug, sucked it up, buried it deep within, and learned how to run...from everything. That *had* to change.

"How did you do it?" I finally asked her. "For all those years, Mom. Do you know how scared I was when you had to walk to work in the middle of the night? Peeling your socks off your bloody heels and tending to the broken blisters. I wanted to make it all better for you somehow, Mom."

My mother heaved a huge sigh. "Honestly," she said, "I have no idea what kept me going except my kids. I tell you, there were times I didn't want to live anymore. I was miserable for a very long time but I'm still alive for a reason. I'm finally drug-free, no more pills and I'm trying to figure it all out, just like you are. Hell, at least you're not sixty and only just getting to it like I am. You got me beat on that one."

We chuckled. I quickly said, "It isn't too late, Mom. I want you to read something I wrote. It's called *When Knives Talk*."

I was having suicidal thoughts after the home invasion and I just wanted it all to stop, to have one moment of mental peace. I didn't want to hurt myself, I just wanted all the noise in my head to stop. Their voices, the smell of their shoes under my nose, the sound of their nylon pants swishing over and over, the sound of duct tape ripping. It was all haunting me constantly. I'd written another poem called *Mommy Please*, in which I described how much I wanted to be happy again, how I wanted her to stop going back to him, and how much my daughter wanted to know her.

I knew my words had touched her deeply when she looked up at me with tears in her eyes. We opened our arms and held on to one another. "Can we just move forward?" I asked.

"That is exactly what we can do." "Let's go for a walk," I suggested. I watched her from several steps behind as we trudged through the snow together. Her hands were buried in the pockets of her thick coat, and her breath came in thin white puffs, wafting past her head and vanishing. We walked along the soft white earth, in silence.

My Mom could not stay through Christmas but she helped us decorate the tree. Each time an ornament went up, more of her defenses went down. It was as if she were melting like a snowman in the sun, and I wished she could stay until there was nothing left of her icy past. In the most magical setting, I caught glimpses of the soft woman buried deep down inside of her when she wasn't panicked or obsessed with survival. There was the woman who had sung and danced with me in the living room of my childhood, filled with hopes and dreams. Oh, how I had missed her! And best of all, her relationship with Breea had begun to flower as we got ready for a very white Christmas in Alaska.

On our way to the airport the day Mom was leaving, she talked lovingly about her hometown of Boothbay Harbor, Maine. I strengthened my resolve to bring her back home one day to face her twisted past. When we'd been there last, just Breea and I, we'd visited mom's high school and looked through the yearbook archives to find her class picture. I'd phoned some of her old friends and met with them, gathering as much information about my mother as I could. I'd even gone to the old house where she'd grown up and the current owner had been happy to guide me through. This was where she ran and played, I thought to myself, back when she was no older than Breea.

When I waved goodbye to my mother, my anger toward her was gone now, and so was hers toward me. As much as I wished she would stay longer, I comforted myself by seeing that the woman who took off for California was in much better shape than when she'd arrived. I knew that as soon as I could, I'd take her to Maine for the first time in 43 years, to her hometown, to the place in which she could re-discover her roots. Most of all, she needed to ask the man she loved most to forgive her her father.

Alaska attracted the weary like a magnet, drawing people who needed to mend which seemed to be the better part of my nuclear family.

I can't imagine we will ever again enjoy Christmas as much as we did that winter in Alaska. The previous year had been filled with terror, but now we were far, far away from the ghosts that had haunted us. Time, distance, and loving family were calming our shattered nerves and soothing our shattered souls. Breea ice-skated on the streets on Christmas Eve and Christmas Day with other people brave enough to weather the bone-chilling cold. We sledded down the hills and had fierce snowball fights. It all seemed so Norman Rockwell perfect.

When Dave called, he spoke in a weary tone, wishing us a happy holiday. He needed help, my help, so I offered him the last of my frequent flier miles to get him on a plane and visit us. Of all the people in my life back home, I missed him and Kristi the most and I wanted him with us. This place seemed to have inexplicable healing powers and new beginnings were something of a theme that season.

As I drove to the airport to pick Dave up, I was aware of how rarely we saw each other when we'd lived only a couple of hours apart. We had grown apart for years before the home invasion and now it had brought us together.

"Hey, Buddy. How's it going?" I asked him as we picked up his luggage at baggage claim. I thought he looked broken and I knew he'd been struggling with a bad relationship for four years. I also knew that his spiritual life was practically non-existent and he was plagued with drug addiction like others in the family. I learned soon after he landed that his employer had just laid him off and he'd been severely depressed in recent weeks. He needed a break and we needed each other. I could relate to his struggle with darkness and drugs but he didn't know that yet.

"You look great, Mi," he said, using my nickname. "Wow, your hair is getting long again, and more blonde." I nodded my head and said, "I'm starting to be someone I recognize." We both knew I was talking about more than my hair color. Dave's trademark bear hug engulfed me, and I smelled his cologne which reminded me of the best parts of home.

"Come here you little cutie," Dave said as he swung Breea around.

"I missed you so much," Breea said as Dave picked her up and smashed his lips into the side of her face.

His attitude right then, amid his depression, was the essence of Dave. He was consistently nice, a guy whom everyone liked, and good-looking enough to catch the eye of my girlfriends when we were growing up. A rugged, outdoorsy man who had always loved fishing and hunting, he would revel in Alaska once his troubles lifted enough for him to open his eyes and look around.

"You okay?" I asked.

"I'm beaten down, Michelle," he admitted. "Thanks so much for getting me up here. If you only knew where I was a couple of weeks ago. But that doesn't matter now because here I am. It was a long flight, so let's go check this place out." With pools of joy welling up in his eyes, he said, "It's so good to see you."

"You too, Dave," I echoed. "You, too."

We talked in the car all the way to Judy's house. He was happy for me that I was doing better and I saw how proud he was when I showed him my diploma. Beyond that, however, he was quiet and he kept to himself at first. I eventually managed to get him out hiking, dancing, and listening to live music in one of my favorite new hideaway dive bar spots with the best fresh Halibut in town. And he seemed jovial when he and Breea built a great big snowman with a real corn cob pipe.

"Why couldn't we have grown up this way?" he said to me when I came out to see their handiwork. Together, we watched Breea pack more snow on the finished snowman, prolonging her enjoyment, unwilling for the project to be over.

Why indeed?

I could see that Dave was getting ready to let his guard down, just like my mother had done a few weeks earlier. Within days, the sparkle had returned to his eyes and his cheeks were a healthy color of pink. In the evenings, we talked late into the night and he began to share with me some of his challenges and personal disappointments. He spoke about how my Mom had shunned him since his early childhood because he was David *Jr.* He revealed his lifelong struggle to gain her approval and how much these problems had wounded him and ruined his relationships with women.

I was stunned when he told me with a quivering chin how much the break-in and the way I'd handled it had affected it. He had seen my life close up for the first time in our adult life and apparently, I had inspired him to change. "I've never seen anything like it Michelle," he said. "Your faith, your courage, and what an amazing Mom you've been through it all. You are such a gift to my life and I just want you to know that."

Now I had something for him. "Do you have any idea that you're my hero?" I asked. You were the only one who came to my rescue when I needed someone the most. I'm so proud to have you as my brother."

"Do you remember when you grabbed that napkin and began to obsessively sketch a picture of you and Breea holding on to one another that day in your dining room at the beach house?"

"Yeah," I replied, remembering those *obsessive* impulses to get the images out of my head.

"Well," he said, "I never told you this but I heard an inner message when you were drawing that said, "*Look, she draws for Me now.*"

I was amazed. He was hearing an inner voice too.

Finally, we got to the nitty-gritty when I told him about my earlier painful and terrifying suicidal tendencies. He broke down and told me that two weeks ago, he was on the floor of his garage with similar thoughts. When I instinctively invited him to Alaska and gave him a free ticket, he stepped away from the so-called ledge.

If anyone understood the pull of 'the ledge,' it was me. And like me, he was the single parent of a child, a son he adored more than anything in his life. But trying to make it all work with an obvious lack of life-managing tools was sometimes more than we could bear. I recalled that earlier that year, I'd had a sense that one day, Dave and I were destined to work together. I'd told him as much, but now I knew in what capacity we would do so. It had come to me back home in San Diego one Sunday morning a few months after the crime. It was an organization I was determined to develop to provide victims of violent trauma with what they needed the physical, emotional, and spiritual support that I didn't get.

I'd gone over my original 'if-only' list.

If only someone had been there for Breea and me to make sure we had timely trauma counseling, a safe place to live, and a home for Charlie, our dog.

If only we'd been told to take self-defense classes to bolster our self-confidence.

If only someone had arranged food deliveries when we were too traumatized to go anywhere or order it ourselves.

If only someone had been there to assure us that our seemingly 'over-the-top' reactions to noises and strangers were normal after such an event!

Not only did we get none of those things. We also remained in physical danger until the gang members who had so severely traumatized us were apprehended. Not an ounce of help or protection was offered or proffered, which sounded like a crime in itself.

Each day, I made my way through enormous stacks of paperwork on how to establish a non-profit corporation. I organized my vision on paper and taught myself how to build a website through trial and error. Then I filed for a 501C3 tax-exempt status. I was on my way. I was also in over my head, but I used the resources I could find -friends, attorneys, clerks and before I knew it, the foundation was approved and ready to roll. And so was Dave.

"Hey, I want to show you something," I said one morning after I'd taken Breea to school. I brought him into the computer room and unveiled the stacks of paperwork I was compiling.

He was amazed. "See what I mean, Mi," he said. "I've never seen anything like it. You are a dynamo."

"Actually," I corrected him, "it's a God thing. And as long as you don't say I have a *dynamite* personality, we're okay."

We both laughed. It felt nice to be gaining back a healthy sense of humor, especially about the crime.

"What can I do to help?" he asked sincerely. And at that, the door to our partnership opened wide.

For the last several days of his stay in Alaska, Dave and I holed up in a twelve-by-twelve room, assembling binders, designing a logo, and printing brochures and business cards. When we took breaks in between our long creative brainstorming sessions, I caught a glimpse of the real Dave playing with Breea, dancing in the snow, gazing out across the vast, brilliant Glaciers, and watching Alaskan eagles soar.

We both quietly wondered where we'd be a year from now. We had a mission and nothing could stop us. When we saw Dave off at the airport, he promised to continue supporting our vision. We both understood our uphill battle. As I watched Dave heading toward Security before he got on the plane, I noticed how different he looked from when he had arrived.

His shoulders were back, he held his head high and he looked refreshed, relaxed, and fit for battle. A fire of purpose burned inside him. It felt like something was shaking my family tree, as the old leaves fell and new ones budded, right before my eyes.

I drove back to Judy's, feeling as if my life were starting to make sense. I passed the snow-covered trees as the landscape stretched out before me. Healing had happened for me and my family in this brave, wild new world. My Mom and I had healed our lifelong conflict and Breea was sleeping through the nights and laughing through the days. Dave and I were going to help people together through music, art, and fashion events and outreach.

The voice inside with which I had previously lost contact, was back, to support me and once again, to become my guiding light.

16

NOTHING BUT THE TRUTH

We hardly spoke on the flight and we went straight to the hotel that the District Attorney's office had secured for us. Painful patterns re-emerged as we entered the vicinity where the crime had happened, but we were no longer in shock and impossible terror, thanks to the year-long stint in Alaska due to court delays.

I was distraught when we both began sleeping badly and Breea clung to me in the night more tightly than she had in months. But even when my sensitivity to strange noises came back, I knew we were doing the right thing. We had to face our demons and those who planted them inside of us on that black, cruel November night.

I left Breea with a close friend while I spent my days pouring over my upcoming testimony and the documents supplied to me by the prosecution. Little did I know that a lifetime of preparation would not have been enough, but Dave was right there, offering to help in any way he could. He even suggested that he move in with us while the trial was on and I gladly took him up on his offer. If there was one thing I'd learned in all of this, it was about asking for and accepting help. I needed Dave;

the closer the trial got, the more troubling the flashbacks and nightmares became.

I knew my work was cut out for me but I was bent on staying positive, tapping into meditation and prayer as a way to stay as calm as I could. With the overflowing physical evidence the prosecutors had in their possession as well as signed confessions from three out of the four accused, it was realistic to expect that we could put these people away for life.

In hindsight, I can see that my greatest strength was my determination. But my greatest weakness was my ignorance as to what defense attorneys were capable of and were allowed to do in open court in front of a jury.

Monday, June 3, 2002

Opening arguments began thirty-one months after the night they attacked us. I clutched onto a picture of Breea that she'd stuck in my hand when I was escorted out of our hotel room. A detective from the prosecution task force led me into an unmarked vehicle that would take me to court and bring me back to the hotel. I'd managed to swallow some oatmeal before I left, but it did nothing for my lightheartedness or my perpetually upset stomach. When I saw the large white courthouse looming up ahead, I could feel the buzz of robed judges, uniformed bailiffs, fast-talking attorneys, and a bunch of bad guys. Nearly a thousand days had passed since these felons had invaded my life and changed it forever. I could feel the anxiety pumping through my veins.

I stared out of the car window, shaking, and settled my focus on my shoes. I needed to get the heel on my left shoe fixed. *Maybe I'm not ready for this.* It didn't matter. This was it. I got out of the car. Even the closing seemed jarring. I tried to regulate my breath as I stepped into the elevator. It was hard to breathe, as if I were in a bad dream, gasping for air, the same feeling I had when we were kidnapped. I couldn't escape then and I couldn't escape now. I was led to a wooden door at the end of a long corridor. The gold engraved sign read Courtroom 17. My escort, a member of the prosecution team, gestured with a swoop of his left arm and I entered.

The room smelled like paper and leather, overlaid with a faint mixture of cologne, aftershave, and carpet cleaner. I passed through the squeaky swinging gate. This was the last phase of an excruciatingly long, drawnout process. In this room. the fate of our tormentors would be decided. I did not want to look up. What if they were already there, standing a few feet away?

To my right, there were empty chairs where the defendants would sit. I exhaled. They weren't in the room yet, but the public defenders were. They must have had no conscience at all to defend such terrible people. I tried to focus on the dozen strangers in the elevated seats at the left side of the room: the jury. They stared back at me, sizing me up like I was an object.

Nearby was Tom Manning, the prosecuting Deputy District Attorney, dressed sharply. When I extended my hand to him, his gaze was gentle and kind. That helped. He moved in an easy, agile manner, consummately self-assured. Just behind him were Detective Rudy Zamora, FBI Agent Jeff Higgins, and Tom's assistant, Dianne. They smiled at me in a way that told me, *"You can do this. Go get 'em, Michelle."* I didn't want to disappoint them. We'd been through a lot together.

"All rise," the bailiff ordered. We stood in deference to the female judge who was entering the courtroom. She looked stern. I resisted a powerful urge to bolt headlong from the courtroom, snapping my attention to the industrial-looking clock on the wall. I took a deep breath. In a couple of weeks, I told myself, this will be over and I can walk around free as a bird, while these men and that misguided woman who helped them would be sleeping on prison cots and eating brown and white food for years to come. That kind of self-talk was how I kept myself calm enough to stay in the room.

I was labeled the "key witness for the state of California." That meant that I would make this one appearance in the courtroom to identify the perpetrators and would not be allowed back until I took the stand. Tom gently took my arm and turned me in the direction of where the defendants were now standing in a line-up. I lifted my head and looked, really looking, at the three men. I nearly smiled when I wondered, how did *they* like being held against *their* will? They were sure as hell not grunting out orders now as they had on that tortuous night.

Christopher Huggins, AKA "Big Hershey," was a massively large man with no trace of emotion on his face.

Robert Arthur Ortiz, AKA "Bones," was wearing professor-type spectacles, his thick dark braids pulled back from his face with a rubber band. If it were possible, he looked even skinnier than I remembered, almost insubstantial.

And there was Christopher Butler, the "talker" and leader of the pack, a badly disturbed man with ugly eyes, who for some reason appeared to want to destroy me. When I looked directly at him, I instinctively stepped backward, my flight response and the memory of trauma that was deeply etched into my brain triggered. I got control of myself. I had a job to do. I needed to identify these male defendants who entered our house so we could go forward with the trial. *God, I wish everyone could see the way they looked that night,* I thought to myself. It took every ounce of my strength and will just to stand still.

"Ms. Renee, raise your right hand please," the bailiff said. I did.

"Do you swear to tell the truth, the whole truth, and nothing but the truth so help you, God?"

"I do, so help me God..." *so help me God.* It echoed across the room and in my mind. I turned to Tom. My throat was closing up and I was trembling uncontrollably. "What do you want me to do?" I whispered.

"Are these men approximately the same height and weight as the three men who violently burst through the back door of your home on November 21, 2000?" he asked me in a strong professional voice.

I nodded and said yes. Then I covered my mouth with my hand. My stomach suddenly felt like I needed to vomit.

"In your opinion," he continued, "are these the men responsible for what happened during that night of terror and what took place the following morning?"

"Yes."

Tom touched my arm and said softly, "It's okay, Ms. Renee. Thank you. You can go now."

Without another glance toward the prisoners, I turned my back and was led to the witness room where I broke into sobs. Breea's picture was now a little crunched ball of photographic paper in my sweaty hands. I opened up the little tight ball, trying to draw strength from looking at her face. I wanted so much to take her pain away, to erase what they had done. I touched the picture softly with my finger.

I sat in the cold stark white witness room for a while, pondering the fact that it had been almost a year to the day that we had escaped with a new identity and more than two years since the kidnapping. The DA had paid our way home and for secure accommodations. But all I wanted was to get beyond this mess and put my focus on creating a new life, a life with purpose and a direction, a life that I was proud of and that Breea could be proud of. I wiped the tears that were streaming down my face, dripping onto the smooth surface of the table beneath my elbows. I tilted my head back and tried to regain my composure while I waited to be driven back to the hotel.

I could hear the words *I believe in you* replaying in my mind. It was Dave's reassuring voice. As usual, he was keeping his promise and he would be there every step of the way, from the beginning of our hell to the last sound of the gavel in courtroom 17.

Dave walked into the courthouse ready to be my ears and eyes. He didn't tell me what they'd said or what the defense had up their dirty little sleeves, for fear of upsetting my fragile state of mind and I didn't ask. I just wanted to get it over with and send the bad guys to jail so we could regain a sense of control. I craved to remember what life was like when we thought the world was safe and we were getting there in Alaska. This had set us back a few rungs on the healing ladder.

Opening statements ended on that Friday afternoon, with everyone prepared to return on Monday to begin testimonies. I woke up on Saturday morning to a gorgeous sunny day in San Diego. A slight haze hung in the pale blue open sky and I peered through the black wrought iron bars on the hotel window. Below, on the pool terrace, Dave, currently 'the snorkeling Instructor,' was teaching his son Shawn and Breea to dive to the bottom of the pool. Then he showed them how to come up to the surface with a furious blow, spouting water into the air. I laughed to see my daughter's tiny face so dwarfed by her snorkeling equipment that only her eyes were visible. She waved at her uncle Dave, carefree and excited to be playing with him and her cousin. I would join in the festivities and make this weekend a good one, leaving everything else behind while I cooked a hearty breakfast for everyone.

I got in the car with my long grocery list and hummed a tune to myself as I drove down the long paved road in the direction of the nearest supermarket. As I walked by the checkout stands on my way to the produce section I spotted the Union-Tribune on the wooden stand. I froze when I read the headline:

BANK MANAGER'S ROLE IN HEIST IN QUESTION

WHAT? I wanted to scream at the top of my lungs. Fighting the urge to run, I read a quote from the defense's opening statement:

"There was no kidnapping here. The bank manager orchestrated the entire crime, was having an affair with the defendant Christopher Butler and is responsible for the theft of $360,000!"

I was being accused of masterminding this nightmare, plotting my daughter's and my kidnapping! I was being blamed for the explosives strapped to our bodies that tormented us still, accused of trying to steal money from my bank and destroying a career I fought and worked so hard for and loved. That wasn't all. Christopher Butler and his attorney were accusing me of having an affair with him! They knew it was a lie. What about the confessions? How could they be allowed to do this? Where was there any shred of evidence to support any of their statements? There could be none because it was all fictitious.

Now I understood why Dave had been so careful to say nothing about opening statements. He knew the defense was trying to involve me in the crime. I looked up from the newspaper numb, disoriented, and outraged. It seemed like my brain had been short-circuited and I hardly knew where I was. For a moment I couldn't locate the door as everything around me started shrinking, closing in until I was so claustrophobic, it was all I could do to breathe in and out.

A woman walked up to me. "Are you all right?"

It must have shown on my face. "How do I get out of here?" was all I could say.

"What can I do for you?" she asked.

"Just show me how to get out of here, please."

The woman pointed and I walked on shaky legs toward the door. I could feel everyone watching me. After I got to the car, I leaned out of the driver's door and threw up in the parking lot. Then I headed for the hotel, with no groceries.

Dave knew something was wrong the minute I entered the hotel room. Breea was taking a shower when I handed him the newspaper that I'd unconsciously taken with me. Now they could accuse me of petty theft, too.

He read it and looked at me with so much empathy, it brought tears to my eyes, and his. He exhaled. "I didn't tell you because I was afraid of your reaction," he told me quite honestly. I understood. The weekend I had anticipated with so much relish had taken a turn in a dark direction. Now the best I could hope for was to just get through it. I held onto my daughter all night long, while she slept beside me.

I remembered Dave's words when the trial was about to start: "Strap yourself in for the fight of your life." The rigid dichotomy is that the DA had a powerful case against them, and their only recourse is to attack me. They went for the jugular, 15 years into my past to destroy my credibility. They had no limits and brought up my sex life, any overdraft I had ever had, my bankruptcy from my divorce, and the debt I incurred after a family member stole my identity. I didn't have the heart to file charges and have her arrested to erase the debt. None of this was explained to counter a venomous defense.

I was told they had no other choice. It happens all the time. They call it 'dirtying the victim.' In our case, since there were no cops to discredit due to so much physical evidence, I was all they had to sink their fangs into.

Once I'd seen the newspaper article that accused me of participating in the crime, Dave stopped trying to save me from the truth, and his observations tumbled out. He described in detail the cast of characters who had been called by the defense to sit in the witness chair. The jury had heard testimony from fellow 'gang bangers', a young black girl named Princess, and Lisa's babysitter who knew about their premeditated plan.

When I thought about it, I could not fathom the fact that Lisa, a mother of three, could have agreed to participate in a crime against a single mother with a daughter. Defense witness scum kept coming and going, Dave told me, with each person more disreputable and despicable than the last.

Finally, it was the prosecution's turn.

Dave walked over to the man who had just taken a seat next to a young hungry reporter and extended his hand. The man stood to shake hands as Dave held him in a death grip. "I'm Dave, Michelle's brother," he said.

The defense attorney tried to free his hand from the human vice without success.

Dave squeezed tighter and pulled the man within an inch of his face and said, "My sister is innocent and you know it. How can you do this to her? You should be ashamed, you fucking dirtbag. How do you sleep at night? How can you live with yourself?"

The man didn't speak and Dave let go of his grip. Then he stepped backward, turned, and made his way out of the courtroom and into the elevator. Close behind him was Detective Zamora. The elevator doors closed and it was just the two of them. "She needs you in that courtroom. Dave," Zamora said. "You have to keep your cool in there. You have to stay calm. Do it for Michelle. She needs you more than ever. I know this is tough but we can't let you back in there if you can't hold it together."

After lunch, Dave returned to the courtroom and sat quietly next to a young reporter who was practically salivating over the salacious details that I would only learn about later. The elated newsman was prepared to slant his articles in the direction of the criminals for one reason only it was lurid, and lurid sold papers.

"No more newspapers, Michelle," Dave said as he grabbed the local morning paper from my hand first thing in the morning in my hotel room. "I can't let you do this to yourself. Now, come on, let's get some coffee."

"Yes, sir!" I said, saluting and getting ready to leave the hotel.

The idea that people were reading trash about me, made me feel ill. We went to the hotel coffee shop, downed plenty of strong black coffee and I waited outside for my ride to the courthouse. By the time an undercover detective named Graham picked me up in an unmarked SUV, I had my game face on.

Herb Weston, the obese attorney who was out to get me in the name of criminal justice, was in the habit of raising his arm in the air and shouting things like, "Isn't it true that you orchestrated this heist, Ms. Renee? You needed the money, didn't you? You engaged in a sexual affair with Mr. Butler and hid the affair from my client, Ms. Ramirez. You know it wasn't my client's voice on the radio that night, don't you Ms. Renee?"

"Do you need a break Ms. Renee?" asked Judge Webber.

I felt defeated, beaten down, and trampled as I faced the stern, kindly-looking woman in robes. "No. I just want it to end. Please can we just get this over with? Please." I wanted to drop to my knees right then and there and beg God, the judge, the defense, and everyone else to make it stop.

I wondered if I was imagining it when I finally heard the defense attorney say to the judge, "No more questions for this witness, your honor." I hardly remember getting off the stand and returning to the witness room. I felt exhausted but also confident when I left the courthouse that day, that the prosecution would win the case. The jury had to be too smart to fall for the lies and false accusations. Didn't they?

The next morning, the last person took the stand Christopher Butler. I thought it was perjury for the defendant to "knowingly lie" on the stand. There were confessions. Why were they not shown to the jury? The judge allowed information to be presented that should never have gotten past discovery because it was irrelevant, untrue, or unsupported. Now my attacker was about to take the stand and lie through his teeth. Still not allowed in the courtroom, I stayed at the hotel, trying to recover from my lashing by the defense. Dave reported to me, especially the surprise arrival of an uninvited guest to the proceedings.

My dad.

For reasons I will never understand, my father had walked into the courtroom unannounced, demanding to be the center of attention. We had told him he was not invited to be in the courtroom because we knew his ego would try to take over the entire room. Pissed, he'd walked straight up to the defense attorney's table and introduced himself as my father holding my work resume in his hand. Almost immediately, Tom quickly moved my dad from the 'wrong' side of the courtroom, directing him to sit in the back row.

My dad also had a few run-ins early in the investigation (big surprise!). He had called the DA and lied about having vital information. When they made time to see him at their office, he had no information about anything. He simply wanted attention and wanted to be the big shot. He was interested in my moment in the spotlight. Something I dreaded but he thought it was glamorous.

Tom called me after that initial meeting and asked me, "What's up with your dad?" He could see why I avoided my father at all costs, the little boy in a man's body, vying for attention from anyone and everyone. Tom tried to explain to my father that he was causing me, and the case, great harm that day in the courthouse. Of course, he paid no attention, but I had an idea of how to get his cooperation.

"Make him feel important," I said.

"Good idea," said Tom. "If we tell him we need him as a potential character witness, he can't stay in the courtroom."

It was settled. They stroked his ego, told him they needed him as a potential witness, and ushered him to the witness room. But it was too late. The other side had already used him to their advantage. As the questioning proceeded, Christopher Butler made up a story about knowing me and referring to my dad being in the courtroom. Of course, he denied stalking me for two long months before the crime, watching me eat, sleep, make love with my boyfriend, take Breea to school, shop at the mall, eat ice cream and God only knew what else. Instead, he spoke about those times as if he were there with us. In his mind, we were an item, lovers, and inseparable. Grotesque!!

When the jury retired to their deliberation room, the next two weeks would be a hell all its own. I was busy deciding whether Breea and I would return to Alaska to live permanently or stay in San Diego. I figured she would want to return to Alaska, but when I asked her, I was surprised that she wanted to stay in California.

"I'm a summer girl, Mommy," she explained. "I miss the beach and the sunshine here. And Uncle Dave and Shawn and Nana. Can we stay? Pretty please?"

Oddly enough, I was feeling the same way. I loved California, too, and I resented moving away because of a pack of gang members who tried to ruin my life. Wouldn't it mean they had won if we moved away? I decided we would stay, but we were still frightened to live alone.

When Dave offered to move out of his girlfriend's house in Ventura and move himself and Shawn in with us, I felt as though our life was going to begin yet again only this time back in our hometown. That night I had a dream:

I was walking through a house with rows of white cabinetry, tile flooring, and a light-colored fireplace, located near the beach.

When I awoke in the morning, I called Kristi and told her about the dream. "This is how it always happens with you," she said. "You must have a direct line to God and you're going to find your place Michelle. I just know it!"

After a few calls, I made a 3:00 p.m. appointment to see a place that we had spotted yesterday from the car. Dave was busy with Shawn and Breea, so I hopped in my car alone and headed to the seashore to meet Mary, the owner of a lovely condo. When I arrived and walked into the small two-bedroom, two-bath condo, I was amazed to see the cabinetry from my dream in the kitchen with the same tiled floor. The fireplace was white, exactly as I'd seen it so I turned to Mary on the spot and told her my story.

"Something is telling me," she said, "to rent this place to you. Don't worry about filling out the application. It's yours if you want it and I'm going to lower the rent by $100.00 a month."

I burst into tears, wrote her a deposit, and went straight back to the hotel, thanking God all the way home. When I brought Breea, Shawn, and Dave to see the inside of the place at 6:00 p.m. that evening, they were relieved we had a roof over our heads. But we were all slightly worried about the size. It was smaller than we had hoped for, a tight fit for sure, but still, it felt right.

"Love grows in small places," Dave said. He knew I was afraid he might bolt after seeing the place.

"Mommy," Breea said, "I like that there are neighbors close by and if something bad happens again they'll hear us this time."

That clinched it. We had found our new home in our old hometown. Now I had something to do instead of pacing back and forth for two weeks of jury deliberations. When Tom Manning finally called, I couldn't imagine how 'one day of deliberations' had turned into two weeks.

"Michelle," he said, "I'm so sorry to have to tell you this but the verdicts are in and have already been delivered."

What? I stared at the phone for a moment like there was something wrong with it. No one, not even Tom or Jeff had summoned me to hear the verdicts. It was unconscionable. "You're kidding me, right?" I pleaded.

"I wish I were," he said in his caring, concerned voice, a voice I suddenly found myself wondering whether I could trust or not. After all, he hadn't called me to court and neither had any member of my supposed 'team.'

"We had no time to call and wait for you to get here," he tried to reason with me. "But I'm glad you weren't here." He was talking faster now, trying to placate my obvious rage that must have been steaming right through his end of the telephone. "I don't know if you could have handled what happened with Lisa."

I held my breath, a terrible numbness spreading through my body.

"She was acquitted, Michelle," he said. "On all charges. She's free to walk the streets. But let's focus on the fact that Christopher Butler, the real bad guy, was found guilty on all charges except kidnapping you. And there's another trial for the other two coming right up."

"What do you mean he was acquitted of kidnapping me? What the hell else would you call it?"

Tom paused for a moment. "One woman juror believed him," he said. "He wasn't acquitted but the jury hung on four of the counts because of that one juror. I spoke to her myself and she said she believed you must have had *something* to do with this. I looked her in the eye and told her that Lisa had confessed. But as you know, her confession was inadmissible and the jury never heard it."

"Why not?"

"Because she and Butler were tried together. He never confessed and since her confession implicated him, they threw it out. But you're forgetting that Butler and the other guys will be sentenced in a month or so and they'll never see the light of day again. Isn't that enough, that they are being taken off the streets?"

No, that was not enough, I thought when I hung up the phone. He was going to jail, so why wasn't I ecstatic? I didn't feel the desired release because my rights had been violated again. The closure I had so anticipated, the satisfaction of seeing Butler and Ramirez convicted in front of me, the entire courtroom, and the press, had been taken from me. How would I have reacted to Lisa's acquittal? I will never know but I resented the implication that I could not have handled it. I was strong enough to go through the experience and to give my testimony. Where did anyone come off judging me as too weak to follow this through to the end?

Two days later, I stared stonily at a picture of Lisa Ramirez on the front page, hugging her sister. The caption read:

Set free and acquitted on all charges:

Lisa Ramirez gets a second chance at life.

At the end of the article, they even mentioned her confession but it didn't matter anymore. I was too enraged and disillusioned to care.

Now it was trial time for "Big Hershey" and "Bones." I had lost all hope of real justice, and when I took the stand for the second time, I steeled myself against the next set of public defenders who were ready to bash me as the first had done. During the second trial, however, the jury had heard their confessions and there was no way to implicate me. They never mentioned me during their admissions of guilt. My boss took the stand in the second trial as well (after I suggested it) and so did our neighbor who took us in that morning. After I testified for six hours, the jury deliberated for one day. This time I was there for the "guilty on all counts" verdict. I felt a sense of triumph, but it was bittersweet.

Lisa was acquitted, and Butler was sentenced to multiple life terms plus sixty-four years. The other two men were each sentenced to three consecutive life sentences plus thirty-two years. After the judge read their sentences, she asked if they had anything to say to the victims. Robert spoke up. Turning his head towards me he spoke. "I'm sorry". He was the only one who showed any remorse or humility.

When I left the courthouse, a little older and a lot wiser, escorted by police past the human rubbish in the hall, I had learned some very important lessons:

I learned that legal defense maneuvering often overshadows a victim's rights under the law. Criminals in our society, even those with signed confessions, are better protected than victims. Victims get repeatedly bashed in the months and sometimes years following a crime, increasing trauma and terror and making healing a distant dream.

There were many tears that day, but unlike in the past, these were tears of joy and relief as I hugged the prosecution team. The press snapped photos of our 'victory' moment. When I left the courtroom and stepped into the hallway just outside of Courtroom 17, the press swarmed me for a further statement.

I looked around for a moment. It was hard to believe that this bustling noisy place was the same hallway I previously had dreaded for its coldness and emptiness. I looked at the swarm of journalists and photographers, practically climbing over each other, microphones extended to catch a statement.

This was the first time I had personally faced these people who had made my pain far worse by printing lies about me to sell papers and get ratings up. But I was surprised to discover that when someone put a microphone in front of my mouth, I was not angry. I was tired of being angry. It took more energy than I was willing to waste any longer. I gave a short statement, trying to describe how it had felt to be accused by the people who had tormented my daughter and me, turning our lives into a living hell. I had left the darkness behind in that infernal courtroom and I was ready to stand on my own two feet. It was time for me to begin helping others through what Dave and I had started all those months ago in Alaska because I knew that helping others heal, even someone I never in a million years expected, was a calling on my life now.

17

SWEET DREAMS

My car was still in Alaska along with most of our things. Breea and I joyfully headed back there to collect what we could, but this time we had a return ticket. Just as the Alaskan frontier had healed us before, by the time our plane landed, we already felt released from defense attorneys, prosecutors, newspaper reporters, and glaring strangers. It was a welcome reprieve.

I had hoped to rent a U-Haul but we were still in a financial crunch so we loaded up the small Kia Sportage with whatever it could hold. A few days later, we packed up the last of our stuff, ready to roll out of town the next morning. I had just gone into the house for the last armload when the phone rang around 4:00 P.M.

My spirits soared when the man from the Social Security office said, "We've approved your case and we have a check for you that includes eleven months of back pay. Can you pick it up on Monday?" "Absolutely!"

We got the check on Monday morning, and by early afternoon, we rolled out of town pulling a U-Haul. It was carrying everything we owned, including the new bike Breea got from her dad for her birthday, and my old mountain bike. Now we could ride our bikes along the way home if the spirit moved us. I got a map and planned the road trip of a lifetime. This time the trip was for us and us alone.

We traveled from Alaska through the mountains of Canada to the West Edmonton Mall, a fabulous place where we sailed down slides in a gigantic indoor water park. We horseback rode and white water rafted in Montana, and finally, we drove through the magnificent beauty of the Redwoods where I had so hoped to bring Breea someday. We were learning more about each other and more about ourselves, discovering how to enjoy life again.

We traveled through small towns and the Grand Tetons. We walked on beaches and waded in rivers. We traveled highways and dirt roads that tossed up rocks that shattered our back window to smithereens. It didn't matter. We loved it all. After twenty-four incredible days on the road, this time staying in bed-and-breakfasts instead of tents and cold suppers, we fell asleep each night with new dreams, and a new passion for life, on our way back to where it all began.

By the time we arrived back in San Diego, we had a brand new lease on life, a new start, and new dreams to pursue. But first I had to know, really know, what went on in the interrogation rooms when all four suspects had been arrested. I knew they had confessed, all but Butler. But what had they said? Who were these people? What happened to them along the way that led them to believe this, what they did to us, was their only option. I had to know.

I drove over to the courthouse and picked up a manila envelope with the confessions, interrogation interviews, disks of all the photographed evidence from the raids and crime scene, partial transcripts, and the FBI 302 reports that contained notes from the scene when I'd given my statement. I was relieved to finally have the papers, but it was two weeks before I got up the nerve to start reading them.

I wanted to be alone to allow the emotions to surface naturally. One evening after Breea had gone to bed, I fixed myself a cup of hot tea, curled up in the corner of my sofa in my comfortable sweats, tucked my feet beneath me, and began to read.

I started with Lisa's confession, given *nine days* following the crime. After I'd read about twenty pages of lies and question dodging, I was surprised to find that starting on page twenty-one, Lisa had started coming clean. She admitted plotting the crime with her boyfriend and said that a friend had snitched on them, hoping to cash in.

My head dropped back onto the cushion. The biggest shock of all was on page 19 where Lisa stated:

"The only reason I lied was to protect Chris," she suddenly admitted.

Indignation rumbled in my gut. In the next few pages, I learned that she and Butler had lived together on Avery Street in a drug house with too many people to count. I looked at the pictures of her house that was raided by the police. It was a disgusting pigsty where no child should ever have to live, let alone three of them.

She went on in her confession, stating:

"I told them I didn't know why people didn't just use fake dynamite when they robbed banks, so they took my advice."

How sick could she be? I read about how they had made the dynamite look real, including a "penny roll" they placed under the tape to make the false explosives look capable of detonating. They had done such a good job on the dummy dynamite that the bomb squad detectives couldn't rule out its authenticity from three feet away.

I looked up from the papers, breathless. Shots of pain traveled from my neck and down my arms from sitting in the same position for far too long. I stood up and stretched, warmed up my tea, and settled back in for more. Lisa described driving them to my house and she said that Bones had provided the two handguns. She said when they'd first arrived at the house the night before the crime, our dogs had barked so loudly they'd taken off. I recalled the coyotes and dogs on the block that had begun baying and shrieking. The thing was, they did that so often, it was hard to determine if there was actual danger, or if they were merely warning a wandering coyote in the night.

So, Breea had been right. There *were* people outside her window when she'd come running to me that night. It was late, dark and I had just tucked her into her bed. 10 minutes later she was yelling for me to come into her room. She sounded frantic. She explained that she saw people outside of her window looking in. I peered out. I didn't spot anyone and brushed it off as the typical coyote sighting in our rural area, coupled with her imagination. I owed her an apology for dismissing her fears the way I had. But if I'd listened and called the police, could we have avoided the worst experience of our lives? Probably not, but I felt awful for having doubted my daughter for even a second.

The next evening, the night when the actual crime occurred, Lisa had dropped them off again. Then I noticed something extremely disturbing on a page of the 302 FBI files. There was my original statement to the FBI at the neighbor's house when I said I'd recognized Lisa's voice on the two-way radio as the woman who had been in my bank. But my detailed description of the crime and who was involved never made it to the grand jury trial. In fact, by the time Joe Barend, the prosecuting District Attorney, suddenly retired and Tom Manning took over the case, the very important fact that I had recognized her voice had gotten lost in the shuffle. Now, right here, Lisa Ramirez herself had admitted, "*The voice on the other end of the radio was mine.*"

She went on about fearing Bones. He was shadier than the rest, she had said, with tattoos on the neck and arms of his emaciated body. She described a hungry look in his eye as if he were a crack junkie. That unstable, shifty man was the one they put in charge of attacking my daughter that night.

At this point in the transcripts, it was noted that the door in her interrogation room had swung open. An agent walked in, telling Lisa that her boyfriend was spilling everything in the next room. He wasn't. It was all part of their tactics, and she retold the story again from the beginning. She admitted that they took about three thousand dollars with them for a trip to Atlanta for the Thanksgiving holiday, the worst holiday of my life. They left the rest of the money at the babysitter's house in a safe they'd purchased at Walmart. But when the babysitter, Cassandra, told them on the phone that the safe had been stolen (which it had), they rushed back to town and were arrested.

I felt a smile form on my lips. I listened to the soothing sound of trickling water from the stone fountain in my living room. I watched the moon shadows dance across the room. I felt sorry for Lisa's children. I just couldn't help it and I prayed that somehow they would be rescued from the criminals who were raising them. I hoped they would someday be transported to good homes with good people who shunned drugs and crime. That was their only chance.

I stretched, yawned, and glanced at the clock. It was 1:17 AM. I was far from finished. I still had the men's confessions to read.

I made myself another cup of peppermint tea, went back to the living room, sat on the couch, and picked up the next batch of papers. I skimmed over Huggins's confession and landed on Robert "Bones" Ortiz's confession which he had given at the very beginning after being pulled from a small crawl space in Milwaukee after America's Most Wanted had profiled the case. His confession was short and anything but sweet:

"As a matter of background," he'd said, "the only individuals involved in the events were me, a black male named Chris Butler, another black male named Chris Huggins, Butler's girlfriend, Lisa Ramirez, and a female named Cassandra Stokes."

I put down his papers thinking about why the two that confessed were not tried first. His confession specifically cleared me of any involvement whatsoever. I was floored by all I had discovered. I returned the papers to my coffee table and allowed my mind to float. As much as I felt contempt for these misguided individuals that had wreaked such havoc in my life, a small spot in my heart was softening from finally knowing the truth. What made these criminals the way they were?

Were they abused when they were young? Was that how they had turned into such bitter, desperate, hostile people?

I lay back against the sofa cushions and closed my eyes.

Robert "Bones" Ortiz's confession replayed over and over in my mind. He was from Santa Barbara, in large part a wealthy neighborhood. I wondered how he ended up so angry at the world. The only one who turned to me to say "I'm sorry" in the courtroom before learning of his sentence had also been the one to clear my name in his confession. Who was he really, deep down? What had happened to him? What made him live so close to the edge that he had just fallen off?

I had closed a long and brutal chapter in my life. I stood and blew out the candles, remembering a promise I'd made to my mother. I would return with her to her hometown and help her complete the healing of her heart. My anger dissolved as I walked down the hall to my bedroom. I watched the peaceful rise and fall of my daughter's small chest, as she lay asleep in my bed. I fully understood how close we had brushed death. I was grateful to be alive and I dropped to my knees beside Breea's bed. "Thank you, God," I prayed, "thank you."

I climbed into bed with her, remembering what I had said to Dave so many times before: *It is all about the message.* I kissed Breea's forehead, thanked God one more time that we had been saved, and whispered, "Sweet dreams, my angel. Sweet dreams."

PART 4
FINDING FINALLY

I know you can see my rawness at this moment. You hear my truth and apology loud and clear. Take it all in however you wish. I only ask that you receive it knowing that I want nothing at all in return.

18

THE LETTER

It was fall in New England, a perfect time to visit Maine and make good on my promise to take my Mom back to her hometown to heal and make peace with her past. Breea and I would be there, supporting her every step of the way and I could hardly wait to show Breea autumn in New England. We boarded the plane, three generations, on an adventure.

Niagara Falls was everything I had imagined. I inhaled with a newfound sense of discovery as I stood on the platform overlooking the falls, delighting in the cold mist, the chilly autumn breezes, and the look of awe on my daughter's face. There was so much for her to learn and discover. Thank God she was alive.

We snapped a few token photos and nestled up in a warm café, sipping hot chocolate, and looking out on the most fabulous view in the world. My mother, never one to open up much and share her innermost feelings, stared blankly. I could see that she was juggling a load of emotions. Her purpose was to find a way to forgive her jaded past, something I wanted my daughter to witness. I'd always imagined a world where forgiveness replaced resentment and now an opportunity lay at my mother's feet.

We rented a car in Buffalo. Feeling strong, I got behind the wheel, happily returning to what I call my control freak tendencies. They seemed to have intensified with the crime, probably because I'd felt so out of control for so long. We drove along, Mom gazing out the window, admiring the tree-lined roads, alive in their annual autumn fire dance. It was nice to see her like this, relaxed and in good health. We'd nearly lost her to septic shock from a ruptured tumor just a few months before this trip. She'd been in a coma for days, underwent major surgery, and had awakened with a new sense of 'being alive.' She, like me, was beginning her ascent out of the darkness.

I marveled at the colors of nature, the tiny purple and yellow flowers that boldly grew in the cracks between the cement slabs of sidewalks. We passed grand lakes, crossed quaint New England bridges and we admired wide-open fields of dandelions that brought a glow of recognition to Mom's face.

We passed flashes of orange, red and yellow leaves wafting down from the heavens, forming radiant blankets beneath the naked trees. Once, we stopped and strolled through the fallen leaves, crunching them under our shoes, cupping and crumbling the colors in our hands. As we got nearer to my mother's hometown, I saw that she and I differed in so many ways. Most importantly, her father had been her hero when she was growing up. Mine had been my enemy.

My Mom was from one of the wealthier families in the small town of Boothbay Harbor, Maine. She grew up in a large house with eleven rooms on an expansive parcel of land with a pond. The intensely cold New England winters brought out the annuals in her mother's garden of Gladiolus. Mom, known for her fiery red hair and unchecked laughter, had been active in her high school in music and drama, living the American dream of the fifties era.

Her dad, the Captain of a 77-foot teak wood and steel sailing schooner, had taken Mom to sea as often as her mother would allow. The vastness of the ocean was my grandfather's passion, something I inherited as my own. All my life I'd heard about my grandfather and my Mom was his pride and joy until a married man entered her life. She'd fallen head over heels in love and had flown straight into the arms of 'unhappily ever after' and gave birth to their love child, my eldest sister, toward the end of their long, life-altering affair. Mom had met my dad when my sister was nine months old. It was a vulnerable time for a single woman with an illegitimate child. I marveled that even though she had a loving father, she still had chosen inappropriate men. It had more to do with circumstances than deliberate choices.

As Mom opened up and told me her story, pieces of my puzzle began fitting together. She talked about my father's brutality and how it had manifested physically and sexually, the extent of which I'd had no real conception. The domestic violence squad knew them both much too well, having come out to our house on many occasions. The school, seeing our bruises, had reported it more than once, but we were always sent right back into the melee, after the cops turned and left, since there was nowhere else to put us. That or the fact that my father had an uncanny and uncomfortable way of charming strangers.

While Breea dozed in the back seat, Mom and I talked candidly about what seemed to be a secret life we had survived. Her eyes brightened each time she released the burden of her secrecy with another story. We even managed to laugh now, sing along to music in the car and connect again in a way that made me feel 10 years old again.

We stopped at stands by the sides of the road with their old-fashioned wicker baskets overflowing with freshly-picked fruit. Crunching, shining Red Delicious apples, and letting pear juice run down our chins. Then she mentioned her suicide attempts. I'd seen her lying in the hospital, but now I was learning why she hadn't wanted to live. In the wake of so much naked honesty, I told her about my romantic exploits, my lover in Cleveland, and my suicidal thoughts after the crime. I no longer needed to save anyone but myself and I wanted her to know me through and through, the same way I wanted to know her.

When we arrived in Maine, our first stop was the cemetery. After a lengthy search for my grandfather's grave, Breea found the headstone carved with "Emery Wilson Howard, Sr." I paid my respects to the man I had yearned to know but had never met. Then I led Breea away, allowing my Mom some time alone with her father. She had a lot to forgive and I hoped she would accomplish her mission so she could stop suffering.

I overheard her prayer: "Please know how much I love you," she whispered as she brushed away the leaves from her father's grave, removing twigs and sticks with great gentleness as if she thought he could feel them. When she left the graveyard, her face shone with a light of surrender.

By the time we left Boothbay Harbor, my Mom had reconnected with old friends, gone back to the house she once called home, and caught a glimpse of her high school. She told me about the 'Glory Days' when she had breathed in that familiar salty fisherman's air. And so, ten days after we arrived, Mom looked and felt like a new woman. Best of all, when we landed back home in San Diego, my mother and my relationship had never been stronger.

The next time I saw my Mom was when she showed up in every way to support Dave's and my new endeavor, The VOW Foundation, DBA Rock to Stop Violence. Our mission and vision were to spread awareness about PTSD as it relates to victims of violence, abuse, and trauma. We were on fire for a message that would inspire youth to become leaders even through adversity and raise awareness by holding music, art, and fashion events that were centered on non-violence and healing for survivors.

With the funds from my back pay, I decided to sink as much as I could afford into launching our organization, getting a group of dedicated individuals together to become board members, volunteers, and organizers. From youth events focused on the principles of leadership at the local Boys and Girls Club to choosing community-nominated makeover recipients who were survivors of violent trauma, we were energized and working around the clock and making headway. Our next move was to organize a full-blown music, art, and fashion event. The first one would be a poker run, then another annual concert at BIGGS Harley Davidson complete with a fashion show, BBQ, and rockin' blues, followed by a sold-out all-star jam at House of Blues featuring AC/DC Drummer Chris Slade and Spencer Davis. Seeking to widen our reach, we headed to Las Vegas for a sold-out show at the famed Black Door owned by the iconic guitarist of "Jane's Addiction", "Red Hot Chili Peppers" and "The Panic Channel".

Non-violent art and rare, classic rock 'n' roll photographs from Morrison Hotel Gallery would line the walls of the venues. Live music played as models walked the runway taking off chains and coveralls painted with words associated with violence and abuse only to reveal underneath messages of healing and empowerment. The visual was powerful. The music was unforgettable and the art simply breathtaking.

The organization and events were getting a lot of press thanks to my background in studying PR. We couldn't afford a publicist so I made up a name, Melissa Rich, got a burner phone, and became our publicist. We were swamped with model calls, venue outreach, art submissions, and band auditions. One band stood out: Fall Into Mourning.

The crowd loved them. They had a great draw and the band members were just really cool guys so when they asked us to meet with them about an idea they had for a music video, we were in. We showed up at a local cafe and sat at a booth next to a window with our friends Rockwell Anderson, who were not only friends of the band but on our board helping us capture all of the events on film.

"We have a song that needs a music video for it." Steve, the lead singer, explained. "We want to tell your story. Maybe a reenactment but focus on all you've done to get to where you are now. More focus on healing and how you are helping others."

I knew the second I heard his idea for the music video exactly what I would do with it visually. The message of healing and no longer hating, no longer carrying anger or bitterness or fear, and deep forgiveness had to be the focus. They agreed and we began to map out how we would accomplish making a video that we hoped would impact the lives of so many who needed to hear and see a message of hope, and witness that there is a way to heal after violent trauma.

Two months later filming began. We adapted parts of the crime to fit the song and include the band in the video. We depicted trauma, PTSD, and how trauma can lead to addiction. But that wasn't all. We depicted a better way to heal, which was not the bandaid from a pill bottle or drinking to numb the pain.

We highlighted the ways we chose to heal. Kickboxing and unloading all of that anger and pain by wailing on a free-standing bag, sometimes with a pinned black ski mask on it. We threw balls as hard as we could at words we had put on a wall, screaming as we catapulted them as hard as we could. Getting out in nature, meditation, and prayer became a cornerstone of our daily life. Listening to disco music and dancing in the living room together, like my Mom used to do with me. Watching only comedies for months to hear the sound of our laughter again.

Finally, after so much work and intention, we let go of all the negatives attached to what had happened and focused on all the positive lessons that we could take forward. To solidify our healing and my commitment to helping others heal, I sat Breea down and asked her about an idea I had.

"The people who did those horrible things to us, how do you feel about them now?"

"I don't know, Mom. I don't think about them that much anymore," she said.

Well, I do. But I think about them differently now. I think about what must have happened to them in their life to have made such a terrible decision. I think about them healing too. Do you think that is possible?"

"I mean, I guess it is. They messed up though."

"I want to write one of them a letter letting him know we don't hate them anymore. Would that be okay with you?"

"I think that's a good idea, Mom."

"Okay then. Let's do it together! It is going to be to the one man who said he was sorry in court. Bones."

"Isn't he the one who attacked me, mom?" "Yes. He is."

"I wish I knew why he would want to do that to anyone, especially a kid."

"Yeah. Pretty messed up stuff. Are you okay writing him a letter with me to let him know he did not ruin our whole life and that we hope he can heal too?"

"Sure. Maybe it will help him."

"I hope so, sweetie. I do. "

We decided to write a letter to Robert "Bones" Ortiz and in the music video, we showed it going into the mailbox as the final scene. It was the actual letter we wrote. We didn't know if he would receive it or read it. How would he feel receiving it? All we knew was that for us, it was time to release it all to God and fully let go of the pain, and the anger and let him know we hoped he could find a way to do the same.

Dear Mr. Ortiz,

Ten years. So much time has passed. I don't know how you will feel reading this but for me, writing this is bringing up so many emotions. Breea is here with me so please know that this is from us both.

Healing has come full circle since that awful night of November 21, 2000, and since that horrible trial where the defense tried to implicate me somehow. Full circle means changing the last memory of seeing you into something so much more powerful than anger; an emotion I no longer have or feel towards you or what happened. I discovered my passion for music again through it all and now organize anti-violence events around the country. A message from you at these events would be amazing.

Another aspect of my healing may come as a surprise to you. You see...I ran away at 15, dropped out of high school, and lived homeless for a time. I ran away because my father was abusive and my Mom was too numb to help herself or us. I worked so hard to make a life for myself, walking away from drugs and starting a career from the bottom. I had beat the odds but the kidnapping broke open in a way that destroyed me yet gave me the chance to rebuild.

I went back to school for my GED and sat in a classroom at a university for the first time at age 35. I am only sharing this because I want you to know we are all human. We make mistakes and fall and if we are lucky we live to get back up. I am standing again, and I hope you are too. I hope you will consider having us visit you so that all of our healing can truly be full circle.

Please reply.

Sincerely,

Michelle & Breea

19

BACK TO DECEMBER

2012

I hung up the phone and stood with my hands in the air, jumping and smiling. I had just booked the venue, 12th & Porter, in Nashville for our next big event. We wanted to expand our reach and after the sold-out Las Vegas show, we knew we could do it in cities across the country. It would take a ton of work and logistic coordination, but to us sharing the message of healing and hope had no state-line boundaries.

The unemployment back pay was running out and the non-profit was still not bringing in enough to pay Dave or me a decent salary to make ends meet. Dave moved out and took on a job with a telecommunications company and I put my PR and marketing chops to the test. It had worked well for our organization, so I figured I could use those results on my resume to land a position with decent pay. Within weeks I snagged a job as a Marketing Director, first for a spirituality enthusiast's dream store in Encinitas, CA., and then for a trendy, upscale hair salon in nearby La Costa. We moved in with a friend to save money for a nicer place and felt the strain of sharing a small bedroom with our two dogs.

I was burning the candle at both ends with my day job, Breea's school, and cheerleading activities and doing all I could at night to keep Rock to Stop on track and ready for our Nashville show. I was not ready for the bright Southern California sun to be shining like a laser in my eyes through the split in my woven beige linen curtains. It's 6:15 a.m. The sun blinded me as I reached up to block it from waking me so rudely.

Rubbing my eyes and stretching my arms out wide, I looked to see Breea sleeping peacefully next to me. I could be blasting loud rock music, or an earthquake could hit, and this kid would still be knocked out cold.

"Hey sleepy head, time to get up."

A grumble was all I got in return. Like clockwork, I headed to the coffee pot and decided on oatmeal for breakfast.

"Look who's alive."

"Morning Mama," she replied and bumped into the counter as she entered the kitchen.

"You look a little pale sweetie. You feeling okay?"

"I feel a little clumsy and have a headache. Probably all the stress from studying for that stupid ACT this Saturday. Not looking forward to that."

"You don't have a fever." I put my hand on her forehead.

"I just need some Advil. I'll be fine."

She gulped down her orange juice with the tiny red pills, finished her breakfast and we both headed back upstairs to get ready for the day. We put on a little make-up, brushed our teeth and we chose casual outfits perfect for a cool December morning in southern California. Then we grabbed two leashes for the last order of business before heading out for our day.

"Come here, Gypsy."

I heard Breea call to the little scruffy terrier she'd had for 8 years. I grabbed my Miniature Pinscher, snapped on his leash and the dogs bounced towards the front door with excitement. Fifteen minutes later, we were rushing back out the door, leaving the leashes on the counter, the dog bowls full, and totally behind schedule.

Breea waved at me and a smile flashed across her face as she disappeared down the street. A varsity cheerleader in 11th grade, she opted to stay away from the drama of high school cheer during her senior year and focus on preparing for college. She got a 3.8 GPA and college cheer tryouts were coming up in March. At 5:00 p.m. she was starting her collegiate cheer training and then she would pick me up from work.

"Thank you for choosing TWIG, how can I help you?" I said as I answered the phone at 12:07 p.m.

"Hi, Mom."

"Hi, sweetie. What's up?"

"I'm going home to take a nap. I am so tired and I don't feel good at all. I've been so clumsy all day, bumping into stuff and dropping things. I don't know what's wrong with me. I think it is just stress or maybe the flu or something coming on."

"Cheer training for college tryouts starts today at 5. You going to make it there?"

"Yeah, I think so. I just need a nap."

"Okay, maybe take a hot bath when you get home. There's some lavender oil next to the tub. Use a few drops of that. It will help you relax a little."

"Maybe. I'll see you around 6:30. Love you."

"Love you too, angel."

With a line of clients standing in front of me, there was no time to think about it for another second.

I looked up at the large round clock on the wall. It was 5:45 p.m., and the day was dragging on. I wondered how Breea's first day of college cheer training was going, and I was anxious to tell her the good news. I had found us a new place to live. It was in the complex we both were so excited about with a resort-style pool, two master bedrooms, and a fireplace, and we were allowed to have dogs.

I took a deep breath in and exhaled loudly, thinking back about the year. It has been such a challenge and Christmas was only 17 days away. Ten minutes later, out of the corner of my eye, I saw someone struggling to open the door to the salon. I glanced up and realized it was Breea. She looked paler than earlier that day as if she'd been drugged. I dropped the day's receipts on the counter and rushed over to her. She sat down on the couch in the lobby with her left leg twisted underneath her as if it was broken.

"Babe! What's wrong? Oh my god, tell me what's going on!" I could hardly keep it together.

"I can't feel my leg or my arm Mommy and I can't...." She could barely speak.

"Okay, okay. What happened today? Did something happen at cheer?"

"No, I didn't go. When I woke up I could barely walk, mom. I didn't think it would be safe."

"Okay, well that's good." I sighed, relieved to know that it wasn't due to being dropped since she is a flier, the one that gets thrown up into the air during stunts.

"Did you go anywhere for lunch? Could someone have put anything in your drink or food? Did you take anything you need to tell me about? You can tell me anything."

"No mom. I promise. I can't see out of my left eye either. Something is wrong."

I tasted burning vomit coming up. My body was rejecting the information I was trying to process.

"Maybe it's a pinched nerve or something. Stress, or...I don't know."

I looked over at my co-worker who was gesturing with her hand, letting me know it was okay to take off.

"Can you walk?" I asked Breea.

"I think so." She was trembling. She could barely move. Once we had left the salon, I stood on her left side, my arms around her, holding her right hip. I practically had to carry her to the SUV. She slid into her seat, I closed the door and I dashed over to the driver's side. She had left the keys in the ignition. My fingers gripped them and turned, the engine started and I tore out of the parking lot, heading for the emergency room.

"Is this something a hot bath might help sweetie? Only you can tell me how you're really feeling. How bad is it?" I wanted so badly for it to be a pinched nerve or stress.

"Mom, I'm so scared. Something is really wrong. I don't know what's happening to me. My arm and leg feel like they aren't attached to my body. Please help me, Mama..."

She began to sob. My eyes welled up with tears. I couldn't make out road signs or stay in my lane. I looked down the main street we had traveled hundreds of times before. The street we drove on to get groceries. The street we drove on to get our mail and shop for bargains at TJ MAXX. The street we drove on to get smoothies and sushi whenever we could afford it. It had a load of stoplights. We'd cracked jokes about them and now I was praying to the Universe that they would, just this once, stay green.

20

NUMB

I didn't care if a cop tried to stop me for speeding. He or she would have to spin those bright lights on top of their black and white car all the way to Scripps emergency room. Nothing was going to get in the way of getting Breea to the hospital as fast as I could. My mind was reeling with so many thoughts and emotions, it felt like a runaway freight train without brakes. I looked over at my daughter. She was leaning her forehead against the window with her left arm lying lifeless on the center divider.

By the time we pulled into the emergency room parking area, it was 6:23 p.m. We had beat almost every red light on the way, thank God. "I'll be right back babe," I said. "I'm going to grab a wheelchair." I flung open my door and bolted towards the line of wheelchairs outside the entrance to the emergency room. I rolled one of them to the passenger side of the car, opened the door, and helped Breea slide into the chair. She was weaker than she was at the salon. There was no way she could hold herself up. Her strength, balance, and ability to stay alert were declining rapidly.

I rushed in through the automatic glass doors and into the emergency room. I went straight to the reception desk.

"How can I help you?" a blonde woman said slowly.

"My daughter can't feel her left leg or arm. She said it doesn't feel like it's attached to her body. She is so pale and..."

She cuts me off. "Any fever, ma'am?"

"Uh, no. I don't think so. She came into my work..."

She cuts me off again. "Any history of drug use?"

"No. She's been tired all day and walking clumsily."

"How long has this been going on?" She turned her head and directed her question to Breea.

"I woke up feeling off," Breea told her. I was bumping into stuff and after I woke up from a nap, it was worse. I can't feel my left leg or arm and I can't see out of my left eye."

The left side of her face was beginning to droop. The right side was moving normally.

"Insurance card please."

"Our insurance doesn't start until the 17th," I said.

"How old is your daughter?"

"Eighteen."

"She'll be financially responsible and needs to sign this paper."

I wanted to scream, *Hey lady, this is serious. Can you get us a doctor? We'll deal with this later!* "This isn't a case of the flu here," I said as I showed her a *give me a fucking break* stare. I jerked the paper out of her hand.

I told Breea to sign the form with her right hand, glad that her dominant side wasn't affected. The ice queen told us to have a seat in the waiting area. In five minutes we were called into triage. A nurse's aide wrapped Breea's arm in a Velcro strap, hit a few buttons, and stuck a digital thermometer in her ear. Her temperature was normal but her heart was racing and her blood pressure was high. The nurse's aide wheeled her into a small room. The sound of the white and blue cotton curtains that hung from silver hooks slid on the metal track and sounded aggressive as it echoed. A nurse entered the room while I was helping Breea onto the gurney.

"Hi, my name is Pam. I'll be your nurse. We're going to run a few tests to see what might be going on. Okay, Breea?" Her voice was warm and sweet, caring, and welcoming calm after dealing with the chilly reception at the front desk.

"The first test is to help us determine if you had a stroke. I need you to put on this gown for me." She handed her a green and white hospital gown that was tied in three places in the back.

A stroke? Oh no. Do teenagers have strokes? I'd never heard of a young person suffering a stroke. I began to unbutton Breea's jeans, tugging at the hem to get them off, and I helped her lift her arms to get her shirt off. As I held up the gown for Breea to put her arms through the holes, she looked at me. Her Caribbean sea green eyes were distraught with fear. Her right arm lifted right away, but her left side only moved slightly. When we were in the car speeding through green lights, although her limbs didn't feel like they were attached, she could still move them. She couldn't lift her arm or move her leg. Less than an hour later, her arm was barely able to move up to where I was holding her gown open.

Instinctively I reached over and grabbed her arm to guide it past the snaps and through the hole. Then I leaned her back onto the gurney after tying three loose bows down her back.

God, please let this be a pinched nerve. Please.

I prayed there would be an easy fix, but I knew it was something far more severe.

The nurse started an IV with medication that was supposed to help keep her calm. Something was triggering her heart rate to spike every time she tried to move. The emergency room doctor stepped into the tight space and introduced himself. He was handsome, young, and spoke calmly. "Now Breea, I am going to ask you a few questions and do a few tests with you right now, is that okay?" "Yeah," she said in a soft baby-like tone I hadn't heard in years. "Can you raise your arm for me?"

We waited for her arm to move. Her face was pinched and her lips were pursed. She was giving it all she had and her arm moved about four inches upward.

"Good job Breea. Now can you raise your leg for me?"

She gripped my hand like a vice and struggled to make her left leg move up into the air. It barely budged.

"You're doing great, Breea. Can you squeeze my hand?" the doctor asked.

She grabbed his hand with her left hand and squeezed. It was a relief to see she could still wrap her long fingers around his. She looked over at me for encouragement. I rubbed her arm, squeezed her hand, and said, "You're doing great, angel. Mommy is right here. It's all going to be fine sweetie." I'm doing what any parent would do in a moment like this. Everything will be just fine."

Of course, it wouldn't. I stroked her long dark blonde hair. I wanted to curl up into a fetal position and render into the floor or crawl up onto that gurney and hold her as tight as I could ... forever.

"Breea," the doctor said, "Tell me when you can feel this on your leg and if it's sharp or dull, okay?"

"Okay."

"Can you feel this?" he asked as he poked her with a sharp pin just below the knee.

"No."

"Can you feel this?" he asked as he ran the dull back of the safety pin down her arm.

"No."

Oh my God, no. No, please. Paralyzed? Please no, no, no.

The doctor looked at the nurse and ordered a CT scan STAT. I am not a doctor but I knew what STAT meant – this was urgent.

"Momma, am I going to be okay? What's wrong with me? I feel numb and I'm scared." Her lips were quivering and curling. She was trying to be brave, fighting to hold back the tears. So was I.

"Yes, baby. You're going to be just fine. The doctor is going to figure out what is going on. Just try to rest."

The nurse delivered the news that it wasn't a stroke. A soft-spoken gentle giant entered the room holding a clipboard. He checked Breea's wristband and promised to take good care of her while they were getting images of her brain and spinal cord. I was not allowed to accompany her so I kissed her forehead as she got wheeled away.

"Love you, Momma," she called out.

"I'm crazy about you. You know that?"

"Yams," she says. She remembered our little inside joke. She tried to smile but the left side of her face didn't move as she disappeared through the double swing doors on her way to get her brain scanned.

How long is this going to take? I asked myself as I paced back and forth. The nurse came into the waiting room and offered me a cup of coffee.

"Yes, please. Cream only," I told her in a shaky voice.

She returned and handed me a paper cup filled with freshly brewed java. I drank it but I couldn't taste anything. She leaned over and touched my back. I glanced into her eyes. I could tell this was bad. This morning, Breea was an 18-year-old high school senior, a cheerleader with hopes and dreams, and plans. Now, she was on a gurney and couldn't move the left side of her body.

The results came back while I was rocking back and forth in the chair next to her bed clutching her hand.

"Ma'am, I'm sorry to say that we found an abnormality in the brain on the scans. We have called a Neurologist. She won't be leaving the hospital for a while." The man said with obvious concern in his voice. Breea was now drugged up and being kept calm and resting to keep her heart rate down. I found a room down the hall, called Kristi and completely lost it. I could barely speak. She couldn't understand me for what seemed to be 10 minutes. A nurse heard me and scurried in with tissues to combat the tears and the snot I couldn't stop from escaping my nostrils.

By the time Dr. Rosenberg arrived at the crack of dawn the next morning, he had studied her scan results. "Ms. Renee," he said. "I'm Dr, Rosenberg. I'll be taking over Breea's case. From what I can see on the scans, it looks like several things could be causing her symptoms. I'm going to order some more tests, including a spinal tap."

A few hours later, I was trying to hold her still, stroke her hair and try to convince her that everything would be all right, something I didn't even believe. Soon afterward, the test results returned with a positive marker for an autoimmune disease known as Multiple Sclerosis. The final diagnosis: Tumefactive Multiple Sclerosis, the rarest form of the disease that presents most often with a catastrophic onset.

Breea was admitted to ICU, and hooked up to more monitors, wires, and tubes. She was unable to speak, hold her head up, walk, or feel the left side of her body at all and she was blind in her left eye. Friends and family started pouring into the hospital, filling up the hallway outside our room with food, balloons, stuffed animals, cards, and blankets.

By day three, the doctor said he believed that she would never walk again. He specialized in Multiple Sclerosis and he'd seen this type of MS onset only once in more than 20 years of studying neurological conditions. The other woman was in her forties when she had an onset and she didn't recover well. But Breea was an athlete. She was so young. She had so much life to live.

When Dave arrived I was a mess. I had broken down on the phone with Kristi and when I saw the wheelchair symbol "handicap" sign on the bathroom door in the ICU, I stopped cold in my tracks and stared at it. I felt paralyzed in my own way. My daughter, my world, was lying on a bed down the hall, barely able to move. The large lesion in her brain and the small one on her brain stem had hit critical mass.

I walked into the bathroom like a robot. I've felt this feeling before. Robotic. On autopilot. It was the same feeling I'd had walking into the bank that morning, being forced to steal money while Breea lay helpless in a closet, duct taped and wired to explode if I made a single mistake. I walked out of the bathroom, grabbed onto a nearby empty gurney, fell to my knees, and sobbed. A nurse helped me stand up and guided me to a room with a chair and she called a psychiatrist.

The psychiatrist suggested something to calm my anxiety. But I didn't want it. For me, pills were the enemy ever since my Mom was hooked on them and they had caused my marriage to crumble. Pills were not an option. She handed me her card and told me to call her if I changed my mind or needed someone to talk to. I needed someone to talk to.

When Dave arrived and asked what he could do, I blurted out, "Get me a bottle of whiskey." An hour later, we were on the curb outside of the hospital drinking out of the bottle that was wrapped in a brown paper bag. "I have to cancel everything," I told him. "The Nashville show. All the programs. This is going to take everything I've got."

"I'll send the email out to everyone," he said, "and cancel Nashville. I'm so sorry Michelle. I'm here for whatever you and Breea need."

We took a few more swigs and headed back in. I was slightly less frayed. My Mom arrived and told me she and Dr. Rosenberg had worked together in a different hospital years before. Acknowledging that Breea was my mom's granddaughter, he contacted the manufacturer of a new, aggressive drug being tested for severe MS symptoms. The hospital couldn't cover the cost so he asked the manufacturer to sponsor the first treatment. They agreed and Breea was wheeled to a building across the parking lot to an infusion center.

Several infusions later Breea began to move her mouth. Two weeks later they moved her to the inpatient rehab ward where she would spend the next six weeks learning to walk again, talk again, feed herself, and pick up objects with her left hand. I left my job at the hair salon and shut down our organization to put my full attention on my daughter. I moved into her hospital room which had a spare bed and two small closets. I never missed a physical therapy session and I used the small computer in the business center whenever Breea was sleeping.

I devoured articles and videos about Neuroplasticity online and exercises to help reroute her brain signals. I became obsessed with gaining as much knowledge as I could about this disease and how to help her beat it. I reported back to her everything I had learned and I decorated her room as if she was at home. I organized pizza parties and football get-togethers in her room, as well as a New Year's Eve gathering with a Martinelli's midnight toast. We played music and kept the hot wax-scented Sensi on constantly. I didn't leave the hospital for weeks. Friends dropped off clothes and when I was running low on clean garments, we secretly headed down the hallway to the laundry room at night with our dirty clothes.

"Is the coast clear" I whispered as she sat in her wheelchair, my fingers women into the handle grooves, balancing a full mesh bag on her lap.

"Yep. All clear," she would whisper back.

Her friends at school organized a fundraiser and her favorite teacher, Mr. Etheridege stopped by with a donation from everyone in his class and a therapeutic pillow. Cameron, a friend of Breea's, dressed in a Santa costume and surprised her for Christmas as her longtime boyfriend flew home from Cornell to be by her side as long as he could. Two girls she cheered with, and had grown up with, Emme and Monica were constants, wheeling her across the street whenever they could for Mexican food and showing up for physical therapy sessions to cheer her on.

Breea and I learned to love Italian ice as we squeezed into a hospital bed next to each other for our favorite shows. My friend Billy, her dad, and I even sprung her out in her wheelchair to hit up a garage sale down the street and wheeled her to a spot that overlooked the ocean. We were making the best out of the worst situation of our life.

"Mom. The kidnapping was a walk in the park compared to this," she told me one afternoon. She had just had a difficult session, trying to walk a few steps in the hallway with her physical therapist.

"It prepared us to be able to handle this situation," I responded. And it had. Who knew that all those years ago, getting through the trauma of the home invasion, kidnapping, and bank robbery ordeal would prepare us for the challenges ahead that we had no idea was coming? Who knew that when I was in high school and I took an ROP course to become a caregiver, a CNA, had been prepared to take care of my daughter?

After 7 weeks, we left the hospital. We couldn't return to the place we were staying because the bedrooms were all on the second floor, so we headed to a friend's house who had a spare room downstairs. We found a foster family for our dogs and began looking for a place to accommodate Breea's wheelchair and mobility challenges. It paid off that I had studied physical therapy and Neuroplasticity and had been present for every one of her PT sessions. I turned the living room into an obstacle course with mini orange cones she could learn to crawl through. I went to Target and loaded up on fun toys that would be great for therapeutic exercises. She was healing, getting stronger, and walking again.

A month later, after staying with friends who had a large spare room downstairs and wide wood floor hallways perfect for her wheelchair, we found the perfect two-bedroom apartment with an attached garage that we could pull into and get her from my SUV into the house in her wheelchair and her new leg brace. We were settling in. I was her fulltime caregiver, and to make ends meet, signed up to become a caregiver for others, too. It was rewarding and difficult at the same time. It took an emotional toll on me and I knew that when Breea recovered enough to take care of herself, I would need to go in another career direction.

I began to think back to the music video. I loved everything about the process of visual storytelling. I knew PR and marketing were a dying breed as the digital era was just beginning to skyrocket into everyone's consciousness. I remembered watching the movie, "The Bridges of Madison County," starring Meryl Streep and Clint Eastwood. I watched in 1995 in awe at Robert Kincaid's character. He was a photographer for National Geographic, traveling the world and taking photographs. I wanted to be him.

When Breea slept, I went back to studying. This time it was videography and photography, consuming hours and hours of YouTube videos on techniques, software, and equipment. In the meantime, Breea returned to her high school campus in a wheelchair, determined to graduate with her class and go to college, I was determined to create a business that would allow me to have a flexible enough schedule to be there for her whenever she needed me.

I dropped her off at school one morning and headed for a local Starbucks on a beautiful sunny morning near the beach in Cardiff, Ca. The things I had learned about videography and my experience in banking, PR, and marketing, would help me start my own business. I began to doodle on a napkin...VERB. Action. Everything in life requires action. Healing and moving forward takes actions, decisions, and choices. It just made sense. I would build a company that reminded me every day that my actions mattered.

I had drawn VERB Media Group on a napkin in a courtyard just outside of a seaside Starbucks on a sunny afternoon in March 2014.

21

WILD GRACE

I hadn't heard this voice in over two years. "Hey, Michelle. You should come to see our new office. We could use some help with PR if you're still in that line of work."

Oliver was a laid-back entrepreneur who had grown a real estate business significantly in the last two years. He and his business partner Sam had called me out of the blue.

"I'm focusing more on videography services," I explained. Studying all those months taught me that traditional PR was dying. I was doubling down on video. I was phasing out that aspect since social media was on the rise and network TV was on the decline. YouTube was harnessing the market.

A week later I visited their new office location. They had come a long way from the past small space with fold-out chairs. The new space was expansive, modern, cool, and fun. I began to visualize how I would tell their story with a camera. This was what I was meant to do.

"What do you think?" Oliver asked. We were sitting in his office, looking out the window that overlooked trees, a greenbelt, and interstate 8.

"Impressive! Congratulations, Oliver. When do you need someone to get started capturing content?"

"Right now would be good," he said with a grin.

The following Monday I had my first gig as a videographer. I didn't have a professional DSLR yet. I didn't care. I showed up as if I had the best equipment money could buy, with my confidence and a creative eye. Within a year I had my own office space there and I was putting their brand and their fun, unique culture on the map. Other people were noticing and began hiring VERB for their events and brand awareness.

Breea had graduated high school and earned her degree in Psychology from SDSU. She had taken a job at TD Ameritrade and moved in with roommates in a beautiful house on a hill overlooking Pacific Beach. She had broken through every treatment and relapsed over and over until a new drug, Lemtrada, was discovered that worked well for patients like Breea with rare and severe symptoms. For eight hours a day for five consecutive days, she received these mild chemotherapy drug infusions. Monthly blood draws for five years showed that her body was handling the drug well and she began to rebound.

Besides a slight limp and some balance issues, she was thriving while I was immersed in growing VERB and moving into my own place for the first time in my life. I'd never decorated just for me before or thought about what only I wanted. I had run away at 15 and lived with someone ever since. Roommates. Boyfriends. My husband and my daughter. Now I listened to music I wanted to hear and I danced in my living room. My inner free-loving gypsy soul was ecstatic! I was living without being Breea's caregiver and her constant companion. Yet, I was still grappling with letting an old identity go and embracing a newer, freer one.

I had a view of the city I love, San Diego, from the 28th floor of a highrise apartment building. Every morning, I sat on my chaise lounge, looked out the window and I meditated, read, and sipped tea from a hand-painted cup that reminded me of my mom. Then I eased into my work day, opening my laptop and checking emails. It was March 7, 2019, when I saw an email that read, "Seeking Contact With Michelle Renee." It had been forwarded to me by my friend, a woman who used to be my manager, Phyllis Parsons.

"Hi, M," she'd written. "I promised I would get this to you... Best, Phyllis."

Below that it read, "Please forward this information to Michelle Renee if you trust that she is open to receiving it. The last we ever want is to open old wounds."

Old wounds? I knew instantly this was not a typical email.

Dear Michelle Renee,

I am reaching out for two reasons.

I have learned via the internet that you have offered resilience work for victims of violent crimes and would be very interested in talking to you about your experience in that work; seeking to understand more about how to support victims/survivors to recover and be on the path of healing.

Secondly and I would imagine more importantly, through my work I met someone who is aware that you have reached out to one of the offenders in your case and you have written him a letter in 2001. He has a letter for you. Please let us know if you wish to receive that letter. We look forward to hearing from you.

Sincerely,
Susan

I was trembling. It had been years since we sent that letter to him, letting him know we were releasing all negativity related to the crime, the break-in, and the attack. We no longer saw him as a monster, but we never knew if he even received our letter. We didn't know if he would ever read it, burn it, or tear it into pieces. We didn't know him or anything about him except what we experienced that night, what we read in newspapers, and what I endured in court.

I responded to Phyllis immediately.

"Wow! Incredible. I can't wait to see where this leads!"

I forwarded it to Dave with a note that read, "I think I'll be visiting 'Bones' in prison...and we'll both be in prison ministry."

Dave had moved up to northern California and had become a member of a wonderful outreach program, Project Heart. They helped people released from incarceration to transition back into life on the outside. They had mentorship programs, and Dave along with his son Shawn hired these men to give them second chances.

I called Breea.

"Hi, angel. Got a minute?"

"Hi, Mom. Sure. Are you okay? You sound different." "I don't know. I just got an email. It's about Raymond." "Oh, wow. Okay. What does it say?"

I read it to her. I had so many questions and I gave Phyllis a yes. We decided that when the letter arrived, we would film it all – going to the mailbox, sitting on my couch with a camera set up on a tripod so we would capture all the emotions.

We got the letter. Our names were written in impeccable penmanship. I held it in my hands for a moment before carefully sliding my finger under the seal. I unfolded the three sheets of white paper, took a deep breath, and began to read out loud.

Dear Michelle & Breea,

I pray this letter reaches both you and Breea in good health and the positive healing spirit as when you wrote to me in 2011. Your letter touched my soul, and reminded me that good people still will amiss of the terrible be good people. For you to write me a letter was heartfelt, but for you to write with the magnitude of emotion, openness, and love was soul felt! I harmed you, Breea, your family, your communities, my family, my community, and I can continue the ripple effect ongoingly. I apologize with all I have in me to you and Breea, your family, community, and any other person, place or thing that was harmed from my actions and/or the ripple effects of them. Your letter helped me dig as deep as I ever had. I sat there while reading your letter and thought, if the shoes were flipped what would I do? How would I react? Could I write a letter? Could I forgive? You're a great woman, a rarity, and I thank the universe for you! You see, while I invaded, crushed, and tore your life apart, you invaded, motivated me, and helped me put my life together. You and your letter touched my soul in a way so deep, I was able to let the tears of sorrow, pain, and shame fall just as they should have. Everything you poured into that letter was and is the fuel I needed to reconstruct myself to the core. You and your letter fueled my construction of self. I had to rebuild on a solid foundation so I could build correctly, strongly, and humbly. You have helped humanize me again and on such a higher and deeper level. You have been and continue to be a huge part in me becoming a better son, brother, father, uncle, grandfather (yep!), and man. So please know that I am grateful, very humbled, and privileged that you no longer see me as the memory of what I was. I have been and still am in awe of you. Yes! you beat the odds, you are standing again and I thank you from my heart soul, and deepest within me for being the spark of my transformation. Last, I will close by asking you a question. If accountability equals responsibility and amends then how can I make amends to you and Breea? You did mention wanting to visit me. I propose a victim-offender dialogue visit through the Restorative Justice Program. I am wanting this. I welcome this, and the opportunity to make amends of any kind. This can be a start.

Sincerely apologetic,
Robert

The sound of the shuffling paper was all I could hear. Seconds later Breea uttered, "Really good."

I stared at the creased pieces of paper in my hands in total disbelief and managed to utter, "Amazing. Just amazing."

"Yeah," Breea responded.

I wiped my eyes. "You know how we always talk about the choices we make that lead to the next thing, to the next thing, to the next thing? Our choice to write that letter and mail it to him restored this man in ways that we didn't even...how could we ever know it was going to come to this, you know what I mean? Anyways, I am so excited. I can't wait to meet him."

"Mmmhmmm." was Breea's typical non-emotional reaction. She usually left all the emotional reactions to me since I've always had enough for us both.

"He sounds incredible."

"Yeah."

"And he sounds intelligent and beautiful in a way. I wasn't expecting any of this. He's in awe of us and he is so grateful. I am amazed. This is what love does. It transforms people. Love heals to the absolute core."

We sat on the couch together re-reading the letter. "Love erases the memory of what was and brings it into what is," I said. "That's what forgiveness does. That is what resiliency does. It helps us no longer see people as the memory of what they were. We are the spark of his transformation after everything he did to us."

I raised my right arm, palm out ready for a return high five. "This could be the greatest thing we've ever done." I kissed Breea's cheek and headed towards the camera to end the recording.

March 10, 2020, 10:51 AM

Happy Sunday Morning.

I wanted to let you know we received the letter. I've read it several times. It is such confirmation that our choice to love and send that letter 8 years ago was one of the greatest decisions we've ever made. The ripple effect of his violent, selfish, desperate actions was great. BUT... The ripple effects of ours, of love, are greater. Love, light, resiliency...is always greater! Tell him it was received warmly, openly, and with great joy of heart and spirit.

See you soon.

Michelle

22

RADICAL FORGIVENESS

Our trip to San Quentin was scheduled for May of the following year. As the world was shutting down due to a global pandemic, so were prisons. No one could visit and our meeting was postponed indefinitely. It seemed like things were going to be under the radar for a while until I received an email on May 6, 2020. The ring leader who continued to lie and show no remorse was up for early parole due to the new laws in California stating that the youth age limit was now 26:

A youth offender is an inmate who was under 26 years of age at the time of their controlling offense and is not otherwise disqualified as a youth offender.

A premeditated crime of this caliber and his prior strikes were not enough for the disqualification criteria. We were asked to write an impact statement regarding this specific offender. Due to his prior criminal activity, his absolute defiance and behavioral issues behind bars, and lack of remorse, our feelings about his release or ever meeting him were the polar opposite of those we had for the man that, from the moment he was captured, confessed, and apologized in court.

When I spoke to the prosecuting District Attorney, he had a plan.

"I'm coming back to work on another case," he said, "and I found out about this parole hearing. I'm going to show up and ask if his testimony was all lies. I'm not holding my breath but I am going to give it a shot." He wanted the truth to finally be told as much as I did but we didn't know how long this guy would hold on to the lies he told about me, the crime, my supposed involvement with him romantically, and being the so-called mastermind behind the scheme. He could take all the untruths he spewed in court with him to his grave. Every vile word that so many would see, read and hear about; Breea's teachers, potential employers, friends, and family. This was the man who perpetrated it, the only one who did not confess. The idea of his being free made Breea and I both feel physically sick.

On June 2, 2020, Tom Manning showed up and asked the question we all hoped would finally be answered truthfully.

HearingTranscript:

DISTRICT ATTORNEY MANNING: I would like to know from the inmate if Michelle was involved in the crime in any way other than being a victim.

INMATE BUTLER: No, sir. She was not involved in any way in the crime. I went into the bank the day before. I went into the bank approximately two months before the crime took place. The first time I went into the bank, there was no intent, there was not even a thought of robbing a bank at that time. And so, I walked to the bank and I was alone on that day. Now, however, later on, the day before the crime actually took place, Lisa went into the bank and tried to open the account without me. She tried to sign my name to document. They told her that I needed to show up. I got upset that she even went to the bank because the plan was already set in motion. We had already went to the house the day before, the, the, the night before. Um, and when I went in there, I sat down and I analyzed, I analyzed the pictures on that lady's desk. I analyzed that she had a child. I analyzed that she wasn't married because I asked her a question. I saw no wedding ring on her hand. I was in full observance of what was going on. And that helped me formulate the plan to carry out that later, later that night or the next day, and Michelle was not involved, no one in her family was involved and I lied and I absolutely lied about her participation in the crime.

DISTRICT ATTORNEY MANNING: I have one last question.
PRESIDING COMMISSIONER SCHNEIDER: All right.

DISTRICT ATTORNEY MANNING: Whose idea was it to put the fake dynamite on the seven-year-old little girl?

INMATE BUTLER: I have to acknowledge that the idea came out when Lisa made the initial statement that, "Why do you guys just walk into the bank with notes? Why don't you just kidnap the family and use dynamite to make, to make the manager go into the bank and give you all the money?" That was the initial idea.

PRESIDING COMMISSIONER SCHNEIDER: Anything else, sir?

DISTRICT ATTORNEY MANNING: I have no other questions. Thank you.

PRESIDING COMMISSIONER SCHNEIDER: So, so, I mean, this whole crime is so terrible and I appreciate Mr. Manning even bringing that out. Of all the horrible things you did, uh, to the victims in this case, what's, what's the worst?

INMATE BUTLER: There was this, there was a slew of things. Uh, I took that lady's peace from her. I took her—

PRESIDING COMMISSIONER SCHNEIDER: Okay. That's not the worst thing. Inner peace isn't the worst. I asked you what the worst was. You can give me the top three, but I don't want to, I don't want you to go on forever. I want you to give me three, three horrible things that you did. Taking someone's peace is not, uh, the worst. Go ahead.

INMATE BUTLER: I threatened to kill her daughter.

PRESIDING COMMISSIONER SCHNEIDER: Right.

INMATE BUTLER: I threatened that if she didn't do what I wanted her to do, that she would watch her roommate die. And I got on the stand and I ruined her credibility when she suffered for years because I am aware that people still wonder if she was really involved in the crime.

By 12:51 p.m. we were pacing back and forth in my living room waiting to hear the decision. At 3:38 p.m. I received an alert that I had a new email in my inbox. It was from Tom.

Mr. Butler's parole was denied for three years. He did admit during the hearing that you had no part in the crime other than that of a victim.

When I received the hearing transcripts in October of the same year I sat alone, trying to find some understanding or compassion. The questions from those nine days on the road to Alaska were still with me. Who were they before this? What happened to them to make them take such a hard turn in the wrong direction? What hopes and dreams did they have? What were their families like?

I wish Butler were more like Robert who had found humility and healing. He hadn't. He wasn't ready to be out on the streets. The psych evaluation didn't support it. His behavior since the arrest didn't support it. The rap sheet he had acquired didn't support it either. He now blamed his then-girlfriend for being the ringleader instead of taking full responsibility for his actions.

As I read the transcript, I learned about his childhood and where he began to take a turn for the worse. My heart as a Mom went out to the mothers of people who ended up like him, behind bars for the better part or all of their adult lives. My mother had ended up there, spending countless days deeply affected by her son's addictions and incarcerations. I decided to hold onto a glimmer of hope that someday he would become more like Robert, choosing to find healing and forgiveness and one day be a free man who would never harm anyone again.

It wasn't long until Robert was up for parole and ready to take responsibility for his actions. We had received letters he had written to us and had spoken to those who witnessed his transformation up close and personal at San Quentin. He worked on himself in prison. He had become a leader in the spiritual program. He was a stellar inmate with outstanding behavior. Because of his honesty and his apology, Breea decided to be present for his parole hearing.

Lockdowns were still in effect so on January 6, 2021, the parole hearing was set up as a video call. By mid-afternoon, my nerves were raw when the call was delayed by three hours. I had a video shoot booked that I couldn't postpone. Breea was on her own.

Two hours into the hearing they asked for Breeas' statement.

Hearing Transcript:

VICTIM RAMSKILL: I would like to make the statement that ever since the victim-offender dialogue that I have had with Mr. Ortiz, I do see that he has worked a lot on himself and has grown and matured and become something bigger than what he was when he committed this crime. And I believe he has done the work and has served the time he deserved for what he did to me and my mom. I am in favor of him being released to go be with his family.

PRESIDING COMMISSIONER CHAPPELL: All right, thank you. Thank you. All right. So the time is approximately 2:42 p.m. We will recess for deliberation.

We were told there was no way he would be released considering this type of crime and that this was his first parole hearing. At 3:07 p.m. they reconvened.

Based on the legal standards and the evidence considered, we find that you do not pose an unreasonable risk to public safety. Therefore, this Panel finds you suitable for parole.

On 4/27/21 at 7:21 a.m., I received a text from someone we knew who was able to be there. The text was a photo that showed Robert with his arms wide open, sunglasses on, and the ocean in the background. He was a free man. After so many years in prison, the thin, wiry, hardened man that once tormented us was gone. Standing there was a man that had changed his life in the most difficult of circumstances. To come out of San Quentin a better man is extraordinary. We wanted to be there but we couldn't be. The conditions of his parole forbade him from any personal contact with us, but this was a new beginning for us all, and that new beginning was about to lead us into a meeting that would change us again. Forever.

April 23, 2022

Dave arrived in San Diego on a short flight from Sacramento.

We were headed to Ventura County for the meeting of a lifetime. When we decided to choose healing and understanding, to 'humanize instead of demonize', it was like the roots of a tree were growing and sprawling out underneath the surface of our lives. It felt as though our choices, listening to the inner voice no matter how loud or how softly it spoke, were producing the fruits of what was right. Those roots had helped me guide my child through recovery in a way that would not further harm her. I had learned that the perpetrators of the crime against us were in a psychological state of prison before they went into a physical one. I came to understand that the human condition is complex and so are the circumstances that drive behavior. Un-investigated guilt, shame, and mental and spiritual abscesses destroy individuals, families, and societies. I was now acutely aware that we can't be healed without a search for understanding, and empathy. I thought about Robert.

I can't imagine waking up in prison, and realizing what you've done to an adult and a child. It was a mammoth level of effort towards healing from that level of pain and brokenness. How could anyone do it? I wanted to ask him directly so we could all learn from each other. Seeing Breea be able to sit down with someone who had harmed both of us so violently, so deeply, would be a remarkable feat. Showing up there with grace, mercy, and love was the greatest gift I could ever give her. I had come to realize that how we show up is what life is all about. Dave was on the same page. We packed our bags for the long drive north. I watched San Diego disappear in my rearview mirror once again. Dave felt the magnitude of the moment. "I've taken a lot of time over the past couple of weeks to make sure that I can be present for this," he explained. "Putting everything aside and shifting it all for this isn't something we get to experience very often. I feel prepared for this. No question."

"We're all as prepared as we can be," I said.

"I went through something similar to this on the flip side," said Dave. "I was an offender who hurt someone badly. I once sat where Robert will be sitting tomorrow."

Dave's thoughts on the way to meet Robert would be spent crossing over to what Robert's journey might have looked like along the road to making amends. He knew Robert had read my first book. Dave too had discovered and read a book written about his victim's journey. They had both read the published work in detail about the consequences of their decisions from those they had wounded beyond most people's imagination. He, like Robert, had spent years in his own hostage situation defined by the silence of words and thoughts they only knew of themselves.

After reading the book 1000 Pieces, written by the man's wife whom Dave had struck with his vehicle on the side of a freeway while under the influence of drugs and alcohol, Dave sent a text to the stamped number in the back of the book. The number was the cell phone belonging to the author, Shirley, the woman he stood next to 25 years prior on Oxnard Blvd while strangers fought to revive her husband, Jerry.

There would be no words other than *I am sorry* as Dave removed his shirt and handed it to Shirley to relay it to the rescue team right before being arrested for manslaughter. Days later he was told that Jerry had survived. 25 years later almost to the date, Dave stood in that same location as he returned to the scene and began to walk back through the entire incident on the way to meet Jerry and Shirley at a small, quaint diner. Before the meeting as the offender, he gripped the wheel and traced the path of the ambulance. He entered the hospital and visited the chapel where Shirley had spent hours, days, praying for her husband. He walked to the ICU and when Dave finally arrived to stand in front of the man he had told himself for years he had ruined, Jerry's first words were, "Don't worry Dave, everything is going to be all right" The same words I heard so long ago in my room that led me to Eagle River.

Dave followed Jerry and Shirley and their pastor to a table to be seated. It was a restaurant, but food was not on his mind. Just as he sat, Jerry reached over and gently put his hand on Dave's arm. "Before you say anything, Dave, I just want you to know I forgave you while I was still in the hospital." Tears welled up. "Now you have to let it go, Dave, you have done it all, you are here, there is nothing more for you to do."

Dave would know Roberts position, feel his nerves and connect deeply to the anticipation entering the room just off of Oxnard Blvd. This time Dave would be sitting in the seat of grace like Jerry had for him. For Dave, and us, nothing else would make any sense other than to understand and pay forward these words. "Now you have to let it go, Robert, you have done it all, you are here, there is nothing more for you to do."

I could see how proud Dave was of our family for how we stuck together through it all, and could now show up in peace, for peace, and share our lives beyond the trauma.

"You carried that around for 25 years?" I asked.

"25 years. I ran from that for 25 years. The pain of being vulnerable. The fear of being vulnerable kept me from really owning what I did."

Facing the truth about the people we have wounded is only one piece of the puzzle. The rest is about unpacking our woundedness like I had begun to do as I drove for nine days. We had a lot on our minds as we passed Sunset Blvd and merged onto the 101 freeway. Breea was quiet. Years passed in between discussions about the *event*. Dave told me once that it had always seemed easier to limit the thoughts, rather than carry them without any real tools to forgive a violation of this magnitude. As we talked and prepared for the meeting during much of the weeks prior, Dave realized how the power of forgiveness had manifested in his own life, and how it was now crossing over to wanting to understand the work and journey Robert had walked. There were parallels in their lives. We all needed to be and feel freedom from our past mistakes and he felt that. We all felt that.

Dave mentioned that the days leading up to the trip were ruled by the thoughts and memories of me and Breea. And although the initial event had long passed, what Dave would think about were the memories of what we had overcome, and how we had redefined our life was something never lost on him. It had all accumulated into another of what has felt like a lifetime of finales. But this was different.

This would be the meeting that would humanize what had felt like ghosts for so long. Today, Breea, a grown woman now, will face her attacker and see his face for the first time. Dave would think about this as only being the design of something Greater... in charge of this moment, for reasons that none of us could fully grasp. The opportunity for freedom. He believed it was going to be the handshake of all handshakes that was only possible from the power of a loving mother who never abandoned the dream to lead with love and to guide her own to do the same. He knew firsthand the fear and the courage Robert had to go through to be in that room. He looked forward to the meeting probably more than any other meeting with a stranger in his life.

"Do you have any expectations, Breea?" Dave finally shifted gears in the conversation and turned his attention to Breea.

"No. I'm just going to see what happens. I have no idea what to expect."

"This is probably very scary for him. He's about to see you for the first time too, without a mask, face to face. How do you feel about that?" She thought for a moment.

"I feel like I'm already past the point of forgiveness. I don't need to hear an apology. I don't need to hear anything. What happened is a closed chapter. This is a new chapter and I'm going to stay open-minded."

"Do you think there's going to be some strong emotions?" he asked her, "I think so, depending on what he says and how he says it." "Okay. I'll have tissues with me," Dave said and we all laughed. He was the king of lightening the mood and asking all the right questions. "Might need a few boxes in a line for all of us to grab," Breea said with a smile.

We drove past a Vons that was a few blocks away from our Airbnb. We decided to stop to pick up a lush, green plant with white budding flowers and a card to go with our gift, a book entitled, *The Upside of Fear* by Weldon Long, a man who spent 20 years in and out of prison and transformed his life to become a successful entrepreneur. We were set to roll into that room, gifts and all. We took some time to get centered in the morning recording how we were feeling as we sipped coffee and tea. Our stomachs were in knots already and none of us slept well. We were going to be late. We lost track of time recording and reminiscing, chatting about the endless possibilities in front of us. By 8:45 a.m. we were on our way to a secure location to meet with one of the men who attacked us and shredded our lives.

We pulled into the parking lot and found a space in front of the dingy tan color building with worn-out brown trim. We saw the older woman who was the coordinator calmly standing there, hands folded in front of her, waiting.

I had thought about this moment for so long and envisioned scenarios that would happen in a perfect world. I never planned for what my body might do. How, no matter the amount of healing and forgiving and choosing what I believed was right, the body would remember and respond. I felt anxiety kick in almost instantly as I reached for the silver door handle. The familiar sense of everything slowing down overwhelmed me. I paused to permit myself to feel this way and to take a deep breath. I needed to reframe my thoughts.

I started telling myself to remember how far we have come in every way. That didn't matter. My guts were twisting and turning and my mind was swarming with thoughts about how all this was actually going to go. The reality of being there began to sink in and I could feel it in my legs. They were unsteady stepping out of the car.

My mind felt blank as I walked toward the old beige building that was in desperate need of a facelift. I suddenly couldn't hear traffic or people talking. My body was already reacting in ways I could never have prepared for.

I noticed Breea's limp was more pronounced as we made our way to the front door. I grabbed her arm gently and she spun to look at me.

"Are you okay?" I asked softly.

"I'm shaking. My left side is starting to feel weaker and numb." Stress was kicking in and triggering a flare-up of her MS Symptoms.

"We don't have to do this, you know. We can leave right now. I would be totally okay with that."

"No. I want this, Mom. It's time."

I knew I had to trust her, trust that this was her decision for herself and not one she was making for me. Still, I felt a pang of guilt and heartache as she limped forward toward the door.

Part of me wanted to bolt. A small part of me even wanted to lunge at him and throw a fist at his face. The other, however, wanted this to be a new beginning full of healing for everyone involved, including him and his family.

The VOD coordinator escorted us into a building with drab décor. A friendly middle-aged woman behind the counter was waiting with sign-in forms while a large, broad-shouldered man stood nearby waiting to take us all up the elevator to the second floor. My heart began to beat faster. I could feel myself begin to sweat under my carefully chosen conservative outfit as we walked down a long hallway. Breea, straightening her back and raising her head, was the first to follow the coordinator into the room. She made sure we knew ahead of time that she wanted to face him first, and speak to him first.

As Breea entered and walked towards the long rectangular table, I saw him sitting on the right side with two other people. They didn't move. They didn't speak. I thought he would stand when we entered the room, gesture to shake our hands maybe. There was none of that. The moment felt as cold as what I imagined a meat locker would feel like. I didn't know what to do as Breea pulled her chair out and sat down in silence. Dave was behind me. He had been quiet since we stepped out of the elevator. It had been so long since the crime he was nearly emotionless. For him it was like walking into a recovery room of people he knew were scared. We were all removed from what Robert had done almost entirely.

I set the bag we had brought for him with a book inside on the table in front of me. I pulled out the generic conference room chair next to Breea and sat down looking him square in the eyes. I studied him briefly. He looked nothing like the man in the courtroom. Nothing like the man in the newspapers, scrawny and sucked up with thick dreads. He looked healthy, and calm, but nervous. Unsure. I wanted to say something but I had no words, and I reminded myself of Breea's wish to be the first to address him. I turned to check on Dave.

I could hear the crackling of the foil around the bottom of the Peace Lily we bought as a symbol of all we had not only hoped for but planned on.

It was the only sound in the room. That moment hung in the balance until Dave broke the ice.

"Can we all hug it out?!" he blurted out. We all stood up and one by one, we embraced each other.

I watched Breea stumble as she reached for him. I could see her struggling to stay upright. My mouth began to water. I was fighting back tears and nausea as I watched him touch her. The man that once held a gun to her head was touching her...again. This time embracing her, telling her how sorry he was. I flashed back to that night. I could still see it all, but I wasn't reliving it.

I felt a familiar sense of freedom as my daughter wrapped her arms around his shoulders. The same feeling I had on the road to Eagle River. I was letting go of the past then. I was healing. I was jumping into new waters. That was all happening again.

When it was my turn, Robert whispered in my ear as we embraced, "I'm so sorry, Michelle."

"Thank you. Thank you for being here."

He moved toward Dave and whispered he was sorry to him as well.

I could see Dave's eyes filling up with emotion. The room erupted in sighs, hugs, and tears as we gave him the gifts we had brought. We sat back down and Breea was the first to speak. "The first thing I want to ask you," she said, "is how are you? How are you doing?"

There she was, the exceptional young woman I raised, facing her attacker for the first time with compassion, forgiveness, and love. There we were, all of us together, choosing to live with our hearts and our souls wide open. There was nothing left but grace.

I scanned the room. My eyes landed back on Breea. My shoulders softened. My eyes teared up and at that moment I knew the greatest accomplishment of my life was unfolding right before my eyes.

EPILOGUE

I had no idea what loving myself meant or how it looked until I was in my mid-thirties, in an old SUV headed up the magnificent west coast into the wide open spaces of the Yukon and Alaska. We had been trapped and terrorized on that terrible night, but the road taught me that I had been held hostage my entire life. It started when I was born with severe asthma. It continued with the childhood trauma, which led to pain, shame, confusion, guilt, and ultimately survival.

When my daughter was born, I thought I could bury my past and focus on being a great Mom and a corporate banker. I could put on a suit every day and hide it all. Every scar. Every doubt. Every self-loathing thought. I believed that no one would ever know who I was on the inside if I disguised myself on the outside.

Then they broke down the door to our home. Guns. Masks. Spears. They broke me. They broke us. I had nothing left to hide behind. I had to prepare to die. Prepare to lose my daughter. Prepare for the absolute worst. But we made it out alive, we were still breathing but was that truly living? What did that mean? How could I be a good mother to a child with so much trauma?

I lay curled up in a ball one night after the attack when I heard a message that shot through me like a meteor in the midnight sky. I sat straight up. There was a presence in my room. A glow. A messenger. "Just rest. Everything is going to be all right. Just rest, and trust."

The nine days I spent on the road toward my daughter in Eagle River, Alaska, were the catalyst for embracing radical forgiveness that became the foundation for the rest of our lives moving forward. It was the launching pad into the unexpected, extraordinary personal growth and spiritual development that my daughter and I counted on for our journey out of violent trauma. I stayed open to trusting the Universe as my guide, embraced what I believe forgiveness is all about as a practice, a release of negative emotions that allowed me to move on from past hurts and resentments and forgive anyone who had wronged me, including myself. I am incredibly grateful that Breea followed my lead.

Today Breea works full-time as an Executive Assistant at VERB Media Group and lives with her fiancé, Steven, in Oceanside, CA. Dave owns and operates a successful Electrician and Solar company with his son Shawn, in northern California. He is also a board member of Project Heart which provides jobs for people needing second chances after being released from prison and/or drug rehabilitation.

My father succumbed to complications related to chronic obstructive pulmonary disease from his years of smoking. The road trip with my Mom proved to be one of the greatest moments we ever shared and we were still talking about it almost up to her final days when she would stop by and bring tea and flowers, two things we both love. She lost her battle with cancer several years ago.

Although not depicted in this work, one of my greatest cheerleaders and soul mates in this lifetime was my brother Ernie who was deeply moved by our journey through the healing process. His life of living on his terms with the pedal to the metal was profoundly light, and dark. His musical genius, his spiritual depth, drug addiction and chosen path of a life on the streets for many years which led to being disconnected for long stretches of time, were fascinating and yet tragic at times to be a part of. His heart was the size of Texas. His ability to retain information, read, and listen was unmatched. He was diagnosed with cancer in 2018 and after helping him live out his final days in a Van and eventually an RV, he passed away in my home in September of 2021. It was the most difficult loss of my life to this point. His time of death was 2:22 a.m. and this book was released as an e-book on 2/22/23 in honor of him.

Another message came through from the VOD. One of the other men involved in the home invasion is ready for the VOD process. We requested a meeting. We are currently in the process of planning our visit to San Quentin in the Spring.

ACKNOWLEDGMENTS

I honestly don't know where or how to even begin putting into words (how ironic is that) those whom I need to thank. First and foremost, I am humbled by what God has done in my life through trusting, listening to divine inner wisdom, and saying yes to a calling on my life that was so much bigger than me, or my story. I am incredibly and forever in gratitude for this adventure called life.

My girl...what we share no words can ever adequately describe or convey. You are my heart, my soul child, my hero. Thank you for being the greatest daughter, support, friend, companion, and my reason for seeking to be better in every way. I love you, adore you, and cherish our relationship beyond measure.

Thank you, Dave, for literally everything you gave and sacrificed for us to be safe, and feel loved, heard, and valued every step of the way. To Ernie, Eric, Debbie, Mike, and Lori, We will forever be a wolf pack in my heart and soul and I am so blessed we all began this crazy journey together as a family.

Thank you Mom and dad for all the lessons, no matter how hard, painful, and heartbreaking it was for us all.

Kristi, Teri, and Kim thank you for never giving up on me and being there when I needed gas money, a place to call home after Breea's MS onset, a shoulder to cry on, and for being the best three people to get me laughing when I needed it most. I love you.

Jana Wilson, my great friend and founder of Emotional Healing Retreats, you helped me give myself permission to go deeply into my childhood woundedness and discover the gift where I only thought there was pain. What a debt I owe you for your work and your friendship, and the gorgeous bottle of tequila.

Linda Panetta, can you believe we met on this wild path on the side of the road in Hope, Canada?! Your words that night, your presence in my life since and our friendship is one I will always revere.

Andrea Cagan, how can I ever repay you for being in my life!? Your guidance, encouragement, friendship, and pure magic as an editor are an immense blessing.

I am profoundly aware of just how much the many calls and texts just to check in on me, flowers, gift boxes, showing up with or sending wine or tea, and cheering me on with gusto helped me stay the course and keep climbing life's mountains. Thank you to every friend who has cheered me on along the way, in so many ways!

To my VERB team and clients who have become friends, thank you for the endless love and support personally, and professionally.

To every musician, writer and producer who has ever made music, the soundtracks of our lives that get us through it all, without your genius, your words and sounds, vulnerability and emotion you pour out for the world to experience, I would truly be lost on this long and winding road we call life.

To the countless strangers who helped me along the way, thank you. You enriched my soul and restored my faith, trust, and belief in kindness again. It is impossible to list everyone whom I am so blessed to have met, spoken to, laughed with, cried with, and traveled with in this life who has inspired, helped, and believed in me in some way. To you all, I thank you.

A NOTE ABOUT THE AUTHOR

Michelle Renee has been featured in numerous magazines, articles, and television segments including Paramount Plus, CBS 48 Hours, Good Morning America, The Huffington Post, The New York Times, Biography Channel, NBC, Lifetime, Investigators and I Survived, to name a few. She has been a keynote speaker at Universities and conferences, a panel guest speaker, and a podcast guest. She lives in San Diego, California. Learn more at Michelle-Renee.com